Find your six.

What if I told you that the ability to find six influential relationships is the only thing standing between you and your biggest goals in business and in life?

That your **revenue** could double or triple if you found the right six? That your search for great **business partnerships** would evaporate if you could uncover six? That you will never want for the right **investors**, **advocates**, and **clients** if you could find your six? And that you could build **a business that you could pass on to your kids or sell** if you could just find those six?

And what if I told you that one of the biggest challenges to finding your six is the lead generation tactics you've been taught? What if I showed you that they are not just keeping you from your six, but simultaneously robbing you of the fulfillment you deserve and make your business vulnerable to disruption in the era of big tech?

Find Your Six is a brief manifesto that shares a new philosophy of how to look at relationships and charts a roadmap for success. In these pages you'll discover:

- **Why lead generation has become a losing proposition**
- **What true influence is and how to win and develop it systematically**
- **How to rethink everything you know about networking**
- **How to never compete for business again while growing your revenue every quarter**
- **How to win back time for the most important people in your life**
- **How to give the gift of influence to others**

Most of all, you'll learn how to identify, win over, and invest in *your* six.

FIND YOUR 6
SIX

STOP LEAD GENERATING
START BUILDING INFLUENCE

PATRICK KILNER

TOWER HILL

Copyright © 2021 by Patrick R. Kilner

In accordance with the U.S. Copyright Act of 1976, the scanning, uploading, and electronic sharing of any part of this book without the permission of the author is unlawful piracy and theft of the author's intellectual property. If you would like to use the material from the book (other than for review purposes) prior written permission must be obtained by contacting the author at patrick@kilnergroup.com.

Thank you for your support of the author's rights.

Tower Hill Press

Library of Congress Catalogue-in-Publication Data

Kilner, Patrick

Find Your Six: Stop Lead Generating and Start Building Influence / Patrick Kilner 1st ed.

ISBN: 978-1-7369120-0-3

1. Business   2. Interpersonal Relations   I. Title

Printed in the United States of America

For Elena,

my greatest influencer

CONTENTS

Introduction.. 1

Prologue 7

Part I: Understanding Influence

Chapter 1: Leading with Authenticity 13

Chapter 2: A Helpful Calamity 29

Chapter 3: Influential Characteristics 45

Part II: Finding Influence

Chapter 4: Landing Influencer Candidate Meetings.... 95

Chapter 5: The Art of the Meeting................................125

Chapter 6: A Table for Six 153

Epilogue 175

INTRODUCTION

It was February 28th, 2008, just a few months before the housing crisis took hold of the country. The red-hot market, in which anyone could buy a home and each home sold was a new record for the neighborhood, had cooled off. Agents in the office, particularly those who had seen hard times before, openly wondered if this time it wasn't just a slower-than-usual winter cycle in the DC area, but the music beginning to stop.

I was the first to the office that morning. The owner of my brokerage startled me with his greeting at the coffee machine. Putting down his bag and taking off his jacket, he smiled broadly. "Hey, young guy! Congratulations!" I could not imagine what he was congratulating me for. Nobody knew we were expecting our third child yet and I was in the office at this hour driven mostly out of a worry about paying my mortgage. I half-smiled. "Eh ... thanks! ... For what?"

Find Your Six

"For what? You sold more volume this past month than anyone in the office!"

For a moment, I was filled with pride. Words of affirmation are my thing apparently. But that wore off in a few seconds. Then my stomach sank as the thought formed in my mind, "If I'm the best in the office over the past 30 days, what does that mean for the rest of the firm?" Reading my mind (or more likely my face), the owner quickly added, "Not to worry. Real estate is cyclical. This company has seen hard markets and we will weather this one too." His voice projected confidence, but I wasn't sure even he believed what he was saying. This market had the inklings of being different than anything this veteran and his company had ever seen. Nevertheless, his bravado certainly sounded better than the alternative.

Unfortunately, I was right and he was wrong. That sinking feeling I had felt at the coffee machine quickly became more of a reality than I could have ever imagined. By the end of the year, agents in the office began to look for new careers, and six months later the company began taking out loans on owner nest eggs to

Introduction

pay salaries. Not long after that the company folded, gracefully taking a buyout from a regional behemoth—something the owner told me he would never consider just a few years before.

More concerning to me at that moment was the fact that I hadn't a clue how I was going to repeat the month I had just had. I was a hard worker, but I could not have told you why I had a great month any more than I could explain quantum physics. For me, closing sales was more of a lucky accident than a predictable event, and I knew I had to find the key to building a business on which I could rely in order to take care of my growing family. As I looked for answers, I watched as the sales of veteran agents shrank, suffocated by the turn in the market. It became clear that those who could count on a strategy for bringing in predictable business were in short supply.

Finding few answers in my local brokerage and determined to find this elusive key, I did what any good real estate agent would do . . . You guessed it: I booked a hotel, hopped on a flight and attended a sales conference! The organizers promised the world if you just followed their failproof system and subscribed to their product—

Find Your Six

more leads than you could ever imagine, the stability of running a great business, and the fulfillment you'd been searching for ever since you didn't get picked for kickball back in 4th grade. This gathering promised to be the silver bullet I needed. (Sounds too good to be true? Well, it was a sales conference after all!)

On the last day of the conference, one of the trainers in a breakout session was describing the optimism a salesperson needs to have and related a joke that President Reagan loved to tell. It was about twin boys. One was an optimist, the other a pessimist. The parents bring their kids to a psychiatrist to get them to be more "realistic" about life. The psychiatrist brings the pessimist to a room filled with toys, but the boy breaks down crying as he laments that if he plays with them, they might break. Then the trainer got to the part about the optimist ... his real objective: "Next the psychiatrist treated the optimist. Trying to dampen his outlook, the psychiatrist took him to a room piled to the ceiling with horse manure. But instead of wrinkling his nose in disgust, the optimist emitted the yelp of delight the psychiatrist had been hoping to hear from his pessimistic

Introduction

brother. Then he clambered to the top of the pile, dropped to his knees, and began gleefully digging out scoop after scoop with his bare hands. 'What do you think you're doing?' the psychiatrist asked, just as baffled by the optimist as he had been by the pessimist. 'With all this manure,' the little boy replied, beaming, 'there must be a pony in here somewhere!'"

The audience roared with laughter. I chuckled ... but not really. Internally I was pissed: "That's what sales is like? Digging through crap?" The joke was a good one, but the application to my business was disheartening (to say the least). "I'm an optimist, but there has to be a better way," I thought. But there was no better way being offered. In fact, everything I had been taught to do at the conference (and frankly in my career to that point) to drum up business had felt like shoveling dung with my bare hands: door knocking, cold calling, mailings, working to increase online lead capture response time, guilting friends and family with "items of value" that they really didn't need. You can only stay excited doing that for so long, no matter how many affirmations you tell yourself. This trainer was on to something—just not

Find Your Six

what he thought. I decided right then that I was not going to look back on a career of picking through horse poop for leads. Not a chance.

What you hold in your hands is not a shovel. Let your competition hang out with the horses. What you have instead in these pages is a telescope—a methodology that will allow you to see with total clarity a path and a future that will not only keep you out of the pony business but will focus you on a far more fulfilling approach to growing your business. I personally employ this methodology and have taught it to hundreds of other professionals in numerous service industries who were tired of how they felt about their businesses and wanted to find a new way forward. Using it allows you to stop digging and instead start building: constructing a business model that gives you a genuine advantage in your market, that survives and even thrives in downturns, and ultimately leads to a career in which, as the leader of your organization, you welcome the day's challenges—all because you learned in these pages that you can't dig your way to success.

PROLOGUE

John had been a past client of mine. He had done very well as a salesperson and sales manager in the printing and document storage industry, but that industry was rapidly changing with the advent of cloud computing. So profound were the changes that humans were becoming largely obsolete in the delivery of the service John was providing. He saw the writing on the wall and reached out to me to see if he could join my company.

I was honored to get the call from John. He had become a great friend and I respected him both professionally and personally. The trouble was that with six kids, John had a lot of mouths to feed, and he had been making good money in his previous line of work to take care of them. At that time, I had never brought on someone who had such a high income to replace.

I had been in business for myself for ten years at that point and had developed a method of generating business that had worked exceptionally well for me. In fact, it was the *only* business development method that

Find Your Six

had really provided for my family and I had never thought about how to teach it to anyone else. Deep down though, I knew that if I could transfer to John the knowledge, skills, mindset and habits that I had used to take care of my family, John could be just as successful.

Regardless of what I felt was possible, the odds were definitely not in our favor: The real estate industry churns through new agents like my teenage boys through a pasta dinner. Less than 60% make it to Year 3 and less than 80% make it to Year 5.

After many long, soul-searching conversations with one another and our wives, we committed: John decided to jump into a commission-only role with my three-person company and I decided that I would do everything in my power to make sure he would not just survive, but vastly outperform the average agent. John needed a banner year right out of the gates to provide for his family.

It was a "burn the ships" moment for the two of us. There was no room for error. We bet big on ourselves, fully aware of the factors that so often claimed the

Prologue

careers of the majority of new entrants to the real estate profession.

How could I *really* ensure that John could achieve massive success? The question kept me up on more than a few nights. I didn't have all the answers, but I knew that transferring my knowledge to John in two areas would be essential:

1) Craft Mastery—the art of providing superb service. Without the ability to provide a service that could compete with and beat the best agents in the area, John would not last long, no matter how good he was at bringing in business.

A focus on training John in craft mastery forced me to create an entire eight-week program that has become our new agent bootcamp. In the years since, the bootcamp has launched the careers of more than a few top producers.

2) Business Development—the art of bringing one's superb service to the marketplace. No matter how good you are at your craft, if you can't effectively trade your service with the marketplace, failure is just around the corner.

Find Your Six

The business development framework I taught John is what you're holding in your hands. The reason I'm sharing it is because it didn't just "work" for John—it's because by every measure he's absolutely crushed it. So have many others I've had the honor to train through the framework that we now call *Find Your Six* (FY6).

This book was born out of my experience in the real estate world, but its lessons cross over into nearly every service industry. In doing the research for the book, I found the patterns you will learn about in these pages in the success of professionals who excelled in tech sales and as trial lawyers, as dog runners and dojo owners, from financial planners to fundraisers. The lessons contained within its pages have worked for me, for John, and for countless others. My hunch is that if you're a master at your craft, the lessons in this book can unlock not only a sustainable business model but deeper personal fulfillment for you as well.

PART I
UNDERSTANDING INFLUENCE

If you are in the game of business, you are most likely a lover of adventure. But what's the cost of setting out on an adventure without the right people and the best possible perspective of the path? Businesses fail because their leaders don't know precisely what—or who—to look for along the journey. The truth is that while a great work ethic and technical expertise are crucial, both will only get you so far. In the pages of this book, I refer to the right people in your adventure as influencers. Without them, every business—no matter the industry, the genius of the idea, or the market factors—is at best relying on lucky breaks to succeed. Influencers will take luck out of the equation of your adventure for good.

Let me be clear about something at the outset. In the age of social media and the rise of "influencers," the

Find Your Six

concept of true influence has become incredibly foggy. Rest assured that this book has nothing to do with getting Bruce Springsteen or Beyoncé to endorse your services. In the first part of this book, you'll find a new way of thinking about influence, the talent behind true influence and, most importantly, you'll understand the cost of *not* finding the specific influencer you need for your business to flourish.

Chapter 1

LEADING WITH AUTHENTICITY

"Every day you may make progress. Every step may be fruitful. Yet there will stretch out before you an ever-lengthening, ever-ascending, ever-improving path. You know you will never get to the end of the journey. But this, so far from discouraging, only adds to the joy and glory of the climb."

WINSTON CHURCHILL

Warning: If you have ever sold anything in the last 40 years, I'm going to attack something that is sacred in the lexicon of sales.

Find Your Six

I'm going to attack the concept of *Lead Generation,* or what is commonly called "lead gen." Every sales role for the past 40 years has been trained in the lead gen mindset. Why? Because it works—or at least it worked for a time. But the heresy I'm suggesting is that it doesn't anymore. Lead gen is a broken concept and it's time you stopped relying on it.

I'm attacking lead generation for three reasons. First, because the way we teach people to do lead gen is no longer a viable business strategy. Second, because it erodes the foundation of trust between you and your future clients. And finally, because there is a better way to bring in business—and it's about the furthest thing from a lead gen paradigm you will find.

The fundamental problem is that lead generation creates a mindset that boils down finding business opportunities into two robotic steps:

Find the lead. Convert the lead.

On the one hand, you might say—just as I used to—that there is nothing wrong with a simple system that produces measurable results. The easier it is, the more repeatable; the more repeatable, the more scalable to a

Chapter 1: Leading with Authority

larger salesforce; the more scalable, the less talented the salesforce needs to be—all without undercutting the fundamental success built into the approach (or so it would seem). These are the reasons why the lead gen approach has persisted for so long.

On the other hand, when you examine it a bit more closely you see that by its very nature the conversion process in lead generation requires very little in the way of new skill acquisition. This flattening of the talent curve is its Achilles Heel, and is why it's often done by machines nearly as well as it's done by even the most skilled script masters on the phone. If there's anything we've learned from the last 40 years it's this: if you find yourself battling to replicate the work that a computer can do, rest assured that technology is going to win that war every time.

Does lead gen still work? Today talented individuals who use the strategy have to spend more hours than ever before to get the same results they used to. If you are satisfied with more work for less revenue, then sure—I won't argue with you when you say that it "works." If you are happy with increased lead spend for fewer and fewer actual leads in your CRM, then by all means "keep on keepin' on." But if you can see that more for less is a losing game in both the short and long run, then this book is for you.

Here's the bottom line: if your business is dependent on a lead gen model, you are fast becoming dispensable when it comes to actually generating business. I want to show you a different path: a path whereby through spending your gift of time, you wind up doing more—and better—business.

A Brief History of Lead Generation

While some might find the news dispiriting that lead generators are on a path to career extinction (like washroom attendants and elevator operators before them), I want you to understand something: lead generation is not synonymous with business development. Lead gen is simply part of the *history* of business development. Mankind bought and sold goods and services for centuries upon centuries prior to the lead gen model.

It may be helpful to imagine business development prior to lead generation as a river teaming with fish of

Chapter 1: Leading with Authority

every shape and size. Imagine professional anglers fishing for business along the shores. They know their craft, what shoreline to stake out at certain seasons and what bait they need to attract the right fish. There was no shortage of fish, anglers had total freedom of how they went about fishing, and because they were masters of their craft, they could not easily be substituted for some new guy with a fishing rod. If the fishing was so good, then why did lead generation become so popular? The thinking was this: instead of the traditional route of cultivating the talent of experts in a field who would then be able to sell their services to clients because of the depth of knowledge they have, what if companies could train people who didn't need to be experts? What if you can eliminate the need for people with intimate knowledge about products and services and replace them with people who know just enough to convince prospects to sign up with the company? The talent a company brought on could just focus on being lead generators, saving years of time (because becoming an expert requires a massive investment of time) and lots of money (non-experts are far cheaper to hire and easier to find). It's easy to see the

Find Your Six

logic of the model and how attractive it would be to a CEO. The concept revolutionized how businesses approached the entire client relationship from generating business to closing the deal.

This was the industrial revolution of lead generation. Think of lead generation at this moment as a dam on the business development river. A dam harnesses the power of a river so that something (typically electricity) can be generated. The new electrical current from this dam was leads—tons of them—funneled to a salesforce like the world had never seen, that made money like they could never have imagined. And so, companies everywhere that were focused on the bottom-line began to replace their anglers with lead generators. They trained thousands of new, enthusiastic sales reps to talk a really good game. Lead generators were trained to memorize scripts ("Good evening! This is [name], calling from XYZ brokerage house…"), learn how to handle resistance ("If I could guarantee you better results, would you be willing to sign with us today?"), and if the prospects asked really difficult questions, they would just pass them on to one

Chapter 1: Leading with Authority

of the few remaining resident experts in the field ("Let me get my supervisor on the phone for you…").

Using this model in the early 1980s, companies quickly discovered that they could also monetarily incentivize their salespeople with far less exposure to the company than paying real experts. There wasn't a business that didn't use the lead gen framework, from kids in tennis shoes selling knives, encyclopedias, and Girl Scout cookies to high-flying executives in Italian loafers selling financial services, real estate, and technology. The beauty of the model was that within just a few months companies could see whether or not a person was good at following the script, handling objections and closing the sale. If not, they could simply bring in more excited, motivated young lead generators. No experts needed here!

Companies had made their sales associates cogs in a big wheel—easily dispensable if the cog did not fit. Sales force hiring, like lead generation, became just a numbers game. As brokerages and agencies and service providers churned through lead gen talent, profits grew. It seemed that the bet on lead gen was paying off.

Find Your Six

Yet the mechanical simplicity of lead generation was (and still is) also its weakness. The lead gen system that, from the perspective of revenue, seemed to be working beautifully in the 1980s and most of the 1990s was horribly disrupted at the turn of the century.

The simple fact is that lead generation was a system designed for disruption from the beginning. In the early days of lead gen, the disruptive forces came from easily acquired new blood who would simply replace old blood in an industry (think Alec Baldwin and Jack Lemmon in *Glengarry Glen Ross*). Managers would praise and incentivize talent that did well and would kick talent that couldn't make quota to the curb. Need to make bigger cuts? Change the quota of calls made. It was that simple. Lead generators have always been dispensable and, therefore, subject to disruption. But understanding why is important: because the communication of basic information is not dependent on the communicator having to acquire any hard skills. If you could "fake it till you make it" with scripts and hard work, you might acquire hard skills and ensure a long, illustrious career.

Chapter 1: Leading with Authority

But if the faking did not work for you, disruption was inevitable.

So it should come as no surprise that as computers became more adept at communicating scripted ideas around the clock to consumers, lead generators across almost every industry—even those who had "made it" before computers—began to lose ground fast. Many even became extinct. Perhaps the greatest example of this is the travel industry. Consider this: how many travel agents do you personally know? Travelocity and its many imitators came to dominate the industry by simply undercutting their disruption-prone human competition, and in short order completely replaced the middleman. By simply being more efficient at distributing information that was once the exclusive realm of the travel agent, computers made them virtually obsolete. The result was cheaper flights, hotels, and car rentals for the consumer and the complete decimation of the travel agent industry. Think of these disruptors as a diverter along a pipeline that rushed leads to travel agents. Once the diverter is installed, there are just a trickle of leads at best left for the agents, eventually shrinking to just a few drops at the end. What was once a relationship that offered the convenience of the consumer not making multiple phone calls was replaced by the convenience of a couple of buttons pushed and the savings of not having to pay an extra human being for the labor.

Charles Schwab and other discount stock trading facilitators diverted leads from financial planners. Sites like LegalZoom can help you prepare simple legal documents, siphoning off millions of billable hours for legions of attorneys. H&R Block and TurboTax soaked up leads, converting the work of CPAs to specialization for wealthy individuals and complex businesses. There's not a service industry that has gone untouched.

Goodbye Lead Generation, Hello…

At the same time that technology has disrupted the human lead generator, it's created a fantastic opportunity for those who have never really felt entirely at home with the lead gen model to begin with, allowing them (if you will) to return to the business development river. The opportunity is only enhanced by the fact that

Chapter 1: Leading with Authority

the millennial generation and Gen Z have grown up with phones in hand, being pitched at every swipe, click and site visited. They are generations that have a highly attuned built-in radar for inauthentic scripts—more than their parents or their grandparents ever had. If it's not completely genuine, millennials and "zoomers" are not interested, and to a person will filter you out and dispense with inauthenticity in literally the click of a button. Good luck trying to sell to these generations with a cold call.

Salesmen like the infamous *Wolf of Wall Street*'s Jordan Belfort may have fooled their parents in the 1980s and '90s, but their kids demand a more authentic experience. Authenticity relies on genuinely deep knowledge and understanding of what it is that you have to sell. If you don't have this, you can't possibly be authentic. There's no more "fake it till you make it" when you're selling to a generation that can smell a fake from a mile away and abhors being treated like a lead. If you are dispensable, the millennial generation will sniff you out. Humanity has a way of getting back to what works: you are either an expert—a master angler—or you're out.

Find Your Six

And here's the even better news for those individuals who are experts: human beings are designed to deeply enjoy being authentic. Want meaning in your work? Don't spend your life conveying data points. Instead, spend it sharing authentic, curated, expert knowledge—ideas that really matter to people and truly impact and protect them, their family, and their wealth. Trade with clients your best ideas—the ones in which you are immersed professionally—such that, without your understanding of how these ideas work, a client simply would not come close to experiencing the benefit you can bring. With terabytes of information at our fingertips, carefully curated ideas are increasingly unique and valuable. They are indispensable wisdom for your client. And they can't be found with the click of a button or through a call center.

What I want to teach you is indispensable business development. It is the furthest thing from lead genera-tion. It's an entirely different mindset—the mindset of a genuine angler who knows where to fish. And if you do it well, you will experience greater fulfillment as well as

Chapter 1: Leading with Authority

greater results with the hours you put into building your business this way.

Choosing Fulfillment

Not long ago I was training a class of 40 business owners. Our focus was a mid-year check-in on their businesses and I walked them through the following exercise:

"At the beginning of the year, you had a plan to generate a certain amount of revenue each month. Write that number down." They quickly went to work.

"Now because we are all optimistic and like big goals, my bet is that you might be lagging in your pace to achieve your revenue goal. Write down what the gap is between your goal and how you are trending year-to-date." A few calculators were pulled up on smartphones.

"Now, in looking at that gap, answer this question: What lead generation tool do you currently have in your arsenal that can bridge that gap by the end of the year? Write the tool down." Within thirty seconds, most had written down their tool.

Find Your Six

"Now look at that tool. Imagine doing that activity three hours every day, 5 days each week, 50 weeks a year for the next three years. How many of you are excited to do that? How about a show of hands?"

I looked around. I waited. **Not a hand was raised.**

Intrigued, I took it a step further: "I'm curious—for those of you who have children or are planning on having kids: how many of you would be excited to teach your son or daughter about this tool you've written down so that he or she could have a more fulfilling career?"

You guessed it. The sky was empty.

It struck me that if a group of experienced, sophisticated professionals felt this way, then there is something wrong with the way we are approaching the topic of generating business. It's not that the solutions they wrote down don't work. It's that the tactics they wrote down do not *fulfill* them enough for them to continue doing them. This is why salespeople have been taught to have vision boards in front of them as they make their calls and even mirrors to check to see if they are smiling before they answer the client: so that they can

Chapter 1: Leading with Authority

trick or distract themselves from the yawning lack of fulfillment through which they are persevering.

What if we choose to do business development in a more fulfilling way?

Chapter 2

A HELPFUL CALAMITY

"Every day is a new opportunity. You can build on yesterday's success or put its failures behind and start over again. That's the way life is, with a new game every day, and that's the way baseball is."

BOB FELLER, HALL OF FAME PITCHER
FOR THE CLEVELAND INDIANS

When I first got into the real estate business in the early 2000s, the lead gen paradigm was still very much the only business development training that existed.

Find Your Six

I was nothing if not tenacious, so I tried every commoditized way you can imagine prescribed by the gods of lead gen to build my business. Here are some greatest hits from my early years:

o Door knocking thousands of homes with small gifts for anyone who would open the door long enough for me to smile and do my best to be endearing.

o Cold calling owners who had withdrawn their property from the market in the hopes that these typically angry strangers would use me since their first strategy to sell had not paid off.

o Employing teams of volunteers to help me hand out American flags to entire neighborhoods (and doughnuts for the kids) on Independence Day (as if I were running for local office).

o Starting at the top of the building and working my way down to the bottom knocking on every door to see when business leases were up—and not infrequently being asked to leave because

Chapter 2: A Helpful Calamity

apparently some people consider this trespassing!

o Calling through all of the people who came to my wedding, who I went to high school and college with, and generally anyone whose phone number I could acquire to see if they had a real estate agent and if they would consider my operation instead.

All of these produced a trickle of business, and I worked very hard at them, hoping to see the trickle turn into a stream and eventually a river. Like most driven, optimistic professionals, I was using every ounce of my natural grit and perseverance on tasks that were high on activity but low on ROI. Amazingly, my broker was giving me awards for producing more than most of the other 90 people in the firm—but what good are awards when you are still wondering if you'll have enough in your bank account for your mortgage payment? The world of lead gen left me with a deep sense of being on a hamster wheel—a lot of movement without a lot of progress. Something had to change.

When the Levee Broke

Then in 2008 the bottom fell out of the housing market. Foreclosures skyrocketed in the DC metro area as well as nationwide. The real estate agent population was cut in half, with NAR membership numbers dropping from around 1.5 million to 750 thousand agents nationwide in only two years. It was the proverbial blood in the streets.

The trickle of business I was getting from lead gen soon turned into the intermittent drips of a leaky faucet. My in-laws mentioned in passing that they could help us financially if need be between jobs and my siblings started to offer unsolicited career advice. I felt like I was on the verge of letting my family down. Finally, my wife took me aside to point out that I had great qualifications to apply for any number of salaried positions. The gauntlet was thrown down—it was time to do or die.

Stress can be an amazing conduit of clarity. The simple truth I realized was this: if I continued to do what all of the agents in the halls of my brokerage were doing, I would never separate myself from the pack. And the

Chapter 2: A Helpful Calamity

pack was being thinned out in a way the industry had never seen.

Many of the agents I had the opportunity to work next to during this time had been in the business for 20 or 30 years. The great majority of them had been top producers and provided well for their families. Many of these veteran experts saw their income slashed in half (or even worse). Several left the industry entirely and quite a few others simply "retired early." They were experts of their craft, but they had doubled down on lead gen, and lead gen was not enough to stay afloat. It was time for me to reinvent myself or pack up shop.

A Conversation that Changed Everything

It was during this time of uncertainty that I picked up the phone to ask for advice. I decided to get into the minds of men and women who had seen their share of adversity in their respective professions. What could it hurt? And if they didn't have advice that would save my business, maybe they would have a job for me.

Find Your Six

One of my first calls was to Gerry, a long-time acquaintance I had always admired. He had a tremendous reputation in the legal field and a long, successful career under his belt. I was desperate to figure out how he had done it. As I dialed his number, fear and insecurity seemed to compound in my mind. What would he think of me? Why should he make time for me? What's in this for him? ... Thankfully, I still dialed. To my great relief, Gerry was happy to oblige and fit me into his busy schedule a few days after my call. We met for about 45 minutes for a quick breakfast before he went to court on a Tuesday morning.

Over an egg sandwich and a side of bacon, I took copious notes as Gerry answered my questions about success in business, his morning routine, his balance of family time, his exercise, and even his thoughts on leisure time. He was a treasure trove of wisdom. I still look back at that conversation and draw the lessons I learned from his sage advice.

But this conversation had something even bigger in store. I had spent the first 40 minutes of our conversation asking Gerry questions that I had prepared. Like a good

Chapter 2: A Helpful Calamity

podcast host who had done his research and knew precisely what he wanted to get out of the conversation, I was inquisitive, thoughtful about the time we had and extracted a lot of value through the questions I asked. But the last five minutes were packed with more insight than I could have ever planned for.

Gerry looked at me, an inexperienced, young pseudo-professional, and said: "You're going to do really well in real estate. I don't know anything about real estate. I make money by taking cases and working my tail off. That's the world I know. But if you come across an opportunity that you think would be interesting for an investor, would you give me a call?"

It's a good thing I had just taken the last bite into that breakfast sandwich or my jaw would have been on the floor. We hadn't spoken about my business plan, about the deals I had done, or even my sales techniques. He had no empirical evidence that I was any good at my profession at all. The entire conversation had been about him, and then all of a sudden there he is telling me that I'm going to do great in my field and asking to have a business relationship.

Find Your Six

Then Gerry looked at his watch and said something even more amazing: "Listen, I've got to head out to make sure I can get to court, but I want to be sure to introduce you to a couple of friends of mine. I'll have my secretary send an introductory email this afternoon. They're great people and even better business owners. I think you'll have a lot in common with them."

As we stacked our trays and refilled our coffee cups to go, my mind was spinning. Gerry not only trusted me enough to propose having a business relationship, but he trusted me enough to put me in front of other business owners who trusted him enough to take a meeting with a total stranger.

I can distinctly remember what I thought to myself on the way back to my car: if I could have one conversation like that every day of my professional life, I knew I would have more business than I could handle.

Influencers that Matter

I'm going to assume that if you picked up this book you have the drive to be technically excellent at what you do professionally. If you don't, stop reading here and go

Chapter 2: A Helpful Calamity

figure out how to master your craft first. I'm completely serious—put the book down now. Without technical mastery of your profession, you will not have anything to trade with the market of potential clients.

After all, it's technical mastery that gives us the confidence to compete and win business. It arms us with the ability never to feel like we are faking it until we make it. But while fundamental, it's not the whole story of success—not by a long shot. Have you ever been frustrated by the realization that comes from knowing your advice, insights and skills are incredibly valuable to clients, but that your business is still not where you know it can be? That there is a gap (sometimes a yawning one) between what you have to give to the market—to clients and customers—and how the market is responding to your ability?

If this is the case for you, you are not alone. Great practices built by great people fail every day because of this gap. We are taught from an early age that being great at something *causes* our success. It's why we spend hundreds of thousands of hours growing our technical knowledge and abilities through schools, books, and the

Find Your Six

imitation of great tacticians. But technical ability will only at best get us halfway to success. While it's an essential and primary element to success, technical excellence is not enough to withstand the constant evolution of your market. Not anymore, and likely not ever.

The gap between where you are today and where you want to go is not just more technical improvement and it's not something that can be bought, like a new CRM or even a good book. Instead, the gap is almost definitely another human being. Not a *what* or even a *how*, but a *who*. Chances are that if you are facing a gap between where you are now and the goals that you want to achieve, you are not looking for a software program or more advice. You are looking for a person who can have a massive influence on your business. You are looking for an influencer.

Driving to the office after my breakfast with Gerry, I started turning over in my mind's eye another question: how many influencers would I need to build a truly sustainable business? A business that would provide for my family in ways that I could only dream of and which would be the envy not only of my colleagues in the office

Chapter 2: A Helpful Calamity

but of anyone in my industry? What kind of professional would I need to be in order to consistently merit the attention of the Gerrys of the world?

Contemplating these questions felt nothing like any type of lead generation or networking models I had learned. If I had treated Gerry like a lead there was no way he would have put me in front of more potential influencers. Not a chance. This was business development in an entirely different arena.

What I would come to find in my journey to discover the right influential relationships to build my business is that the number of influencers to which the average person organically has access are few and far between—and yet there is no shortage of influencers with whom you can connect when you have a method to uncover them.

I also unsurprisingly found that not every potential influencer for my business would deploy his or her talents and contacts into helping me. Some influencers simply had a different vision, sense of urgency, or needs for their business than I had. I also discovered that while true influencers often held positions of authority and power, not all of them lived at the top of the company organizational chart. In developing the systematic approach for finding influencers, I even learned to identify influencers whom earlier in my career I would have dismissed. Most importantly, I learned that just the right handful of key players for a business can change the entire course of a firm and at least one person's professional career. They did for me, and continue to do so.

Family Matters

As the father of a growing family, I was around needy and vulnerable people every time I came in my front door. The way I saw it, when I stepped out the front door each morning, my obligation to my family was to go and spend time with influencers. I created a rule for myself as a result of this realization: ***Guard your professional time, effort, and money for the MOST influential individuals so that you can guard your personal time, effort, and money for the MOST vulnerable.***

When I finally understood this truth, my level of frustration went down significantly because I didn't

Chapter 2: A Helpful Calamity

need to generate tons of business from my friends and family, my classmates and teammates, the people on my wedding list, the people on the sidelines of my kid's soccer game, and the people I would see at church and share a coffee with on Sunday mornings. Once I realized that these weren't typically the influencers I was looking for, I was freed up to focus on the people who were. And it made being with the people that I love and enjoy spending time with far less anxiety-inducing.

Gerry set the bar for me early in my career about the type of person I knew I needed to find. In Gerry I had found an influencer **completely by accident**, so my next task was to figure out how to find these influencers **completely on purpose.**

At first, I had no playbook for finding influencers— just a deep conviction that I needed to have more Gerry-type conversations. So, I picked up the phone and scheduled as many face-to-face meetings as I possibly could. In the early days, I met with almost anyone. If you would give me the time of day, I would buy you coffee (and by the way, it really was a cup of coffee—not breakfast or lunch and certainly not over happy hour,

Find Your Six

because those get expensive when you're having three meetings a day).

Over the course of a year I had almost 600 face-to-face meetings. During this time, I learned what questions to ask, the type of industries to investigate and, most importantly, the kind of person I was looking for. At the beginning of my year-long odyssey, I thought that by sheer volume of meetings my business would grow, but I came to see that what really moved the needle were just a few key individuals. While it's undeniable that everyone is potentially influential, in terms of my business less than 1 in 20 people I met with ultimately had the impact I was looking for. It turned out that was enough—in fact, that number was more than enough. Luckily, you don't have to have hundreds of meetings to figure out who will be most integral to growing your business. That's what this book is for. You can thank me later for saving you from a caffeine addiction and thousands of dollars spent on gas and lattes. Instead, you can concentrate on those individuals who are located at the peak of what I call the Influencer Pyramid.

Chapter 2: A Helpful Calamity

THE BASICS OF THE INFLUENCER PYRAMID

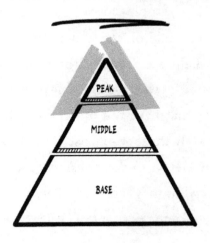

Conclusion

There are all sorts of amazingly gifted people in this world. The vast majority of them have little to no influence on your business and therefore comprise the base of the Influencer Pyramid. They aren't bad people or unimportant—in fact, it's likely that most of your friends and family will be categorized at the base. But for the purpose of growing your business, they are just not that influential. Then there's the middle of the

Find Your Six

pyramid—not the most influential people, but not the least either. These people too are good people and maybe even people you rely on when it comes to your work. They might help keep your firm running, but their impact is limited, as we'll see in the next chapter. In terms of influencers that have the power to truly grow your business, it's only those who exist at the top level of the pyramid—the Gerrys in your business life—even if you don't know who they are yet. These are the most influential people: the peak influencers.

This book is about finding them.

Chapter 3

INFLUENTIAL CHARACTERISTICS

"It is not the brains that matter most, but that which guides them—the character, the heart, generous qualities, progressive ideas."

FYODOR DOSTOEVSKY

Where are the peak influencers? How can you find them? Before you can answer either of those questions you need to know how to identify them. While they're not exactly hiding in the tall grass, nor are they self-promoters—they're too busy *being* influencers.

Find Your Six

What's more, there are all sorts of influencers with varying degrees of influence. You probably don't have the time for over 600 face-to-face meetings. Is there a way to narrow down the great mass of influencers to identify peak influencers?

While influencers come in all different shapes and sizes, my experience (and the experience of the 600+ professionals I interviewed) kept leading me back to three fundamental characteristics that peak influencers always had. These fundamental characteristics may at first seem very limiting when you sort through the influencers you know or the people you meet—and they are. After all, you are not looking for just anyone. But at the same time, honing in on individuals who have these qualities surprisingly opens up new avenues and opportunities to discover influencers—people you might not have thought likely candidates for the label. These characteristics will serve as guardrails along your Autobahn for identifying the individuals you need to know in order to successfully build a business. And since driving a high-performance vehicle on a superhighway takes some practice, as you apply these rules of thumb

Chapter 3: Influential Characteristics

to your search for influencers you will discover nuances in how to use them in your search for your peak influencers.

Characteristic 1: Putting in the Time

Perhaps the most tell-tale characteristic of those individuals who will reside at the top of your pyramid is longevity. I'm not talking about longevity in terms of the number of years someone has been at a firm—the type of longevity people get gold watches for. That is often longevity by inertia. The type of longevity I'm talking about is the length of time a professional has spent with his or her clients. Where there is professional longevity with clients, there you will find peak influencers.

Think about it on a personal level. The friends who have had the greatest influence on you are the ones who have put in the hours with you. Those late-night phone calls or long drives. Letters expounding on ideas just to make sure that you understood where they were coming from. They are the ones that will show up at your funeral if you happen to go first and the ones who will comfort your family. Friendship, just like professional trust, is

Find Your Six

anchored in hours spent cultivating a relationship over time. There's really no substitute.

Obviously some professions have an easier time cultivating long-term relationships than others. It's really tough to clock a lot of hours with your clients when your job is selling fast food or in a retail shop. The more transactional the relationship, the less contact you have and therefore the less influence you can have. Of course, you can provide "white glove" treatment in transactional settings, but what should be clear is that this treatment does not generate the type of trust I am talking about. There are also plenty of professions you might think are tailor-made for relationships built on longevity—financial planners and family doctors, pastors and attorneys, social workers and coaches—but where many individuals never dig in with their clients to really get to know them and their needs. In those instances there is a failure to use the built-in client interaction time to cultivate a relationship. Simply put, it's entirely possible to spend time with people without earning their trust, whereas longevity in the hands of a peak influencer

Chapter 3: Influential Characteristics

makes all the difference when it comes to actually *having* influence.

Peak Longevity

Years ago, I built a professional relationship with a young attorney who had an amazing ability to refer business to me. His client relationships would endure for years. At first, he might be hired to take care of a tax issue for a firm, but the trust he built would lead to the firm asking his assistance to create new business entities, restructure employment agreements and ultimately assist with mergers. Thousands of hours of work would pass over the course of years. With each new problem solved for the firm, his influence would grow. While he had clients who would hire him for a discreet, short-term engagement—perhaps to review a document or form an LLC—his greatest influence was with clients with whom, in his own words, he had the opportunity to work for a minimum of thirty days. The result of his longevity on my business was seen in a steady flow of new clients referred by him. Needless to say, this thirty-day rule

Find Your Six

intrigued me and I began looking for it in other professions.

In my industry, many high-producing real estate agents have relationships with local home builders who tear down old homes and erect multi-million-dollar replacements. If you cultivate the relationship with the builder and prove your value, you can earn some high dollar commissions. This seemed to prove the 30-day hypothesis since the builder spends well over a month with most clients. But try as I may, I was never able to find the right builder relationship.

Disappointed, but convinced that I could forge great relationships in the builder arena, I wound up connecting with another group of professionals in this industry who spend 30 or more days with their clients: sales representatives at larger national builders. Most real estate agents assume that the rep makes the sale after a meeting or two with the customer and that's the end of the relationship. But in fact the most successful reps are engaged with the client for months, helping to pick the lot, guiding decisions on the finishes in the home, assisting with financing, and even connecting them with their new

Chapter 3: Influential Characteristics

neighbors. They had a 30-day relationship with their clients as well—and that 30-day increment wasn't an endpoint for the relationship but rather the tipping point.

Because they put in long hours with these clients, their influence was significant. So when these clients needed to sell their previous home, the sales rep was trusted implicitly—and those reps handed on my name as a resource. In just 18 months, my business doubled in the form of referrals as a result of this transfer of the client's trust—and over the years it has accounted for millions of dollars in revenue for my team. While not the owners of the companies, many sales reps turned out to be exponentially more influential than I would have ever imagined. One veteran rep described for me a 30-year relationship he had with a client as they moved four different times, each time reflecting a particular life circumstance. It wasn't just that the client didn't want to reinvent the wheel with each purchase; it was that the rep was invested in their happiness and was trusted to make the transition to their next house seamless. The rep wasn't just "repping" the builder—he was also representing the trust of the customer.

Find Your Six

Where Longevity Resides

Even the owners of retail shops or small restaurants can have influential longevity. They may have regulars who come in, but their greater influence is on their employees who depend on them to take care of them, keep a shop open, and help them find shifts so they can go on vacation. Oftentimes it is on these employee relationships that owners/influencers will have greater influence than on the people who purchase their goods, especially when they spend less than a month with their typical clients. In this sense, an owner's truest client is his or her worker.

Everybody has Clients

Let me pause here to offer a brief note about the term "clients": I'm using this term as a catch-all for the people with whom an influencer has longevity. In that sense, a pastor has clients with whom they spend lots of time: the parishioners or the faithful of the congregation. Clearly the pastor doesn't call them clients, but they certainly are those individuals over which the pastor

Chapter 3: Influential Characteristics

exercises his influence. A homeschool co-op mom who leads classes at her house and helps develop curriculum for other families has clients in a similar sense. She may not get paid for her involvement, but people look to her year after year to provide a service and she spends hours of time with the other parents who are seeking out this brand of education. A fundraiser at a non-profit also has clients: the individuals whom the fundraiser asks for money. And if fundraisers are good at their job, they also spend a lot of time with their coworkers developing relationships and relying on their expertise to land a major gift from a client. Both coworkers and the major donor are receiving influence.

During my year of interviews, I began categorizing the professionals with whom I met and discovered that they coalesced into three layers that formed the Influencer Pyramid:

- o At the base of the pyramid were people in professions who had less than a day of contact with a customer, client or constituent. This category constituted a majority of the people I

Find Your Six

knew: people in retail, in transactional sales, in call centers and in food service. These were the occasional handymen, the Uber drivers, and the substitute teachers. Many did their jobs with excellence, but their job simply did not put them in contact with clients long enough to have significant business influence.

o In the middle of the pyramid, I uncovered another large group of professionals who spend more than a day but less than a week with their clients. They had more influence than the base of the pyramid on their professional relationships because of the time they spent, but it was a limited kind of influence. This category held almost every service profession I knew: attorneys, doctors, real estate professionals, tax preparation, financial services, chiropractors, personal trainers, and yes, even politicians. Some of these were naturally restricted by the length of their time with clients, but a great many of these could have invested more time but chose to focus more

Chapter 3: Influential Characteristics

on getting the deal done and moving on to the next prospect.

o At the top of the pyramid, I discovered professionals who typically invested more than a month of work with their clients. These were the professionals who have the greatest influence on their professional relationships. These were truly the *peak influencers*. As we've seen, these professsionals had chosen to stake their professional reputations on a different approach.

AVERAGE LONGEVITY OF CLIENT INTERACTION

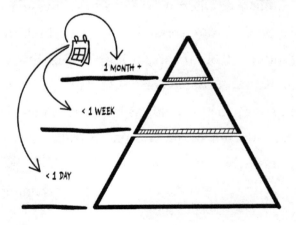

Find Your Six

Valuing Longevity in Yourself

I began to search for these peak influencers religiously. Once I saw the influence of their relationships, it became clear that, if I was going to build an enduring business, the most efficient use of my time would be to find peak influencers. Longevity was the first piece of the puzzle to discovering who was truly in this category.

Once longevity was identified as a key characteristic, it served as a lens through which I was able to see with striking clarity the potential influence of a person. It also served as a lens through which I could see myself. Was I a peak influencer when it came to time invested with clients? My profession certainly *could* lend itself to this type of influence, but if I was being really honest, I had to admit that I was not passing the 30-day threshold with my clients as often as I could. As I immersed myself into what real influence meant, I came to realize that peak influencers did business with other peak influencers and that longevity was a critical ingredient in becoming an influencer.

Chapter 3: Influential Characteristics

With my team, I took a deeper look at all of the investments of time that we made into clients—from before they had signed on with us formally through the buying or selling process and into the post-transaction phase as resources to them after a sale. We rethought every aspect of our client interaction to increase our personal investment, our value-added interactions, and thus our influence. Over the years, the professionals who ended up being able to refer me the most were the professionals who, similarly, spent over a month with their clients. Some professionals had served their clients and their clients' parents. That's generations of time invested with others, and I came to realize that the "Est." dates on companies weren't just quaint affectations but deeply meaningful signifiers.

Influencers Talk

Time spent is invaluable when receiving a referral from an influencer with longevity. You are working as an extension of an influencer when you receive business from them. Often, the knowledge that they have is fundamental to how you will work with their referrals.

Find Your Six

These are not just handoff and "forget about it" referrals. Their professional reputation is on the line. Influencers with longevity want their clients to continue to receive influence—after all, that's why they continue to be influential.

This is also why with influencers you report back. You let them know that the people they've entrusted to you are being cared for—that you are investing the time. Without breaking client confidence, you make sure that an influencer who has put their trust in you and who connected you with their referral knows that you are handling their people better than even they would. That's how you keep the referral flood gate wide open.

If clients are everywhere, then influencers are everywhere as well. Peak influencers are those that have longevity in their relationships with the people who rely on them. If you choose to build a business that is non-transactional—that becomes a long-standing asset as a result of the influence you have on your clients, employees, partners and which withstands the forces of disruption—you need to understand this simple rule:

Chapter 3: Influential Characteristics

peak influencers attract and do business with other peak influencers.

Characteristic 2: Showing People Matter

Longevity is fundamental for peak influencers, but as alluded to above it's not just putting in the time that matters. The second fundamental characteristic that pervades a peak influencer's long-term relationships with clients is *trust*. And just as longevity isn't simply spending time, this trust isn't just any kind of trust.

Over the course of any given day, we all trust hundreds of people in small, transactional ways. We ask someone for the time and trust that person won't lie to us. We eat food prepared by others and trust that it's not poisoned. Each time we get into a car, we trust the other drivers on the road will observe the rules of the road. While it's clear that the breakdown of trust at any level can prove to be catastrophic, the myriad of transactional situations we encounter each day don't require a deep form of trust—just the faith that everyone will act in ways we can predictably rely on.

Find Your Six

Then there's the kind of trust that's a step above the transactional. It's a sort of bonus over and above mere transactional trust. It's rewarding to know that your home inspector is taking an extra careful look at the roof and the HVAC system and a perk when the waiter at your favorite joint brings out a free cup of coffee without you asking. It's an added benefit when the bank teller waives the fee for an overdraft and an outright gift when your hairdresser sends you home with a free bottle of a favorite shampoo. Not surprisingly, we value this trust and these professions may benefit from the bonus of your satisfaction in the form of a tip, or a Yelp review, or perhaps a recommendation to a friend. But your tip will not make or break their business, nor did their actions raise their influence to the point of being a peak influencer. You didn't have to trust them with your children or your family heirloom or your sanity to receive the bonus service, nor did your show of appreciation for the service have a significant impact on their earnings, professional prestige, or the trust the next client has in them. But to be clear, this is not to say that

Chapter 3: Influential Characteristics

these professions can't act in ways that create trust and make them peak influencers.

How would they have to act in order to reach the pinnacle of the Influencer Pyramid? When it comes to the trust peak influencers generate, it is something categorically different from transactional or bonus level trust. It's not the momentary trust needed for obeying traffic laws or the transactional trust needed at your favorite burger joint. It's not even the bonus trust that you have in the tree service that you hire to remove a dead limb looming over your house. The trust that peak influencers establish is more akin to the trust a child has in his parents, a protégé's trust in her mentor, or the trust you have in that friend you can call on for anything at all. When this type of trust is broken, the impact can feel (and in some cases actually is) irreparable. The long hours a hairdresser puts into a relationship with a client can result in that kind of trust just as, over time, I have come to trust a particular house inspector to whom I refer all of my clients.

The Cost of Failure

A useful way to begin identifying the kind of trust peak influencers generate is in terms of the concept of opportunity cost. Economists speak about opportunity cost as the foregone benefit that you would have derived had you chosen one path over another. Applied to trust, we can think of the opportunity cost of a failure of trust by asking the question: "What is the opportunity cost of a breakdown of trust between... ?" When applied to professions, the lost benefits of a rupture in trust are far greater in certain professions than in others. Consider what is the opportunity cost of a breakdown in trust between

... a consumer and Amazon Prime Video?

... a customer and the waitress at the diner?

... a parent and a child's teacher?

... a client and his attorney?

... a business owner and her CPA?

Chapter 3: Influential Characteristics

Clearly there are professions in which a breakdown in trust results in a more catastrophic outcome than others. You need to trust your hair stylist, but even if he completely messes up, the results, while embarrassing, are not particularly catastrophic (although if you get enough of these disconcerting trims, you might just take matters into your own hands and opt for my hairstyle). It's definitely preferable to trust the bakery that makes your graduation cake, but it's not a complete disaster when you open the box and read "Congratulations on your retirement, Bobby!" Hair grows back. Cakes can be re-iced and refunds made. In fact, memories are made from such instances when transactional trust didn't pan out. But if you can't trust your attorney, your surgeon, or your best friend, you have a serious problem. The opportunity cost of an erosion of trust in these instances is massive: some things just can't be made right when they go wrong.

If this deep level of trust is essential to influencers, then how do we identify it? Two qualities of this kind of trust can serve as a test of someone being a peak influencer.

Find Your Six

Fiduciary Fidelity

One quality of the kind of trust that peak influencers have is fiduciary care—a deeply held obligation to maintain fidelity to those they serve. The responsibility to remain steadfast and faithful in the support of a client is something that only a small portion of the population is called on to *legally* deliver. Attorneys have a fiduciary obligation to their clients. Financial advisors also have fiduciary law that governs their client interactions. Real estate professionals do as well. Each of these professions by law has to represent their client's interests above their own as long as the client's interests do not break the law. But what of the professions that do not legally have this obligation? Can individuals in those roles take on the responsibility of a fiduciary? You bet.

Fiduciary responsibility is found in the little league coach who spends the extra half hour working on ground balls with the clumsy kid who won't ever help him win a championship. It's the rabbi whose fiduciary responsibility to the needs of his congregation gets him out of bed in the wee hours of the morning to make a home visit and

Chapter 3: Influential Characteristics

pray with a family. It's the owner of a company that retains employees over the long haul because she's constantly looking out for their best interest: finding projects at which they will excel, helping them grow in their professional capacities, and taking interest in their family life.

A friend of mine in the legal services industry once told me about a lady who works at the front desk of a big law firm downtown. She knew everything about the firm: where the partners liked to dine, if they were having marital problems, if their kids were sick, what their calendar was going to be four months in advance, and (most importantly for my friend) if they were frustrated with their current service providers. She was indispensably good at her role—efficient, detailed, dedicated—and the attorneys relied on her for nearly everything. She wasn't just trusted as a result—she had earned their fiduciary trust.

Habitual Fidelity

It's entirely possible for any of us to exercise what seems to be fiduciary responsibility in one-off situations.

Find Your Six

But peak influencers also have the quality of being *habitually* trusted. Fidelity is a function of track record, since fiduciary trust is built over time by showing that you are trustworthy.

If you've ever needed dental work, you want a dentist with a track record of serving people beautifully for years. A while back my family dentist told me that I needed to visit a specialist for a root canal—not news you want to get, and honestly a procedure that is rife with horror stories. She gave me the referral and within a week I was in the chair, mouth wide open, staring at a table of mini-power tools. The doctor proceeded to ask me questions about the pain I was feeling for what struck me as an inordinately long time—ten minutes or so. Then he took another ten minutes to carefully reexamine me. And then he did something utterly surprising: he wrote down some exercises I should do daily and sent me on my way, convinced that my pain wasn't in my tooth but actually caused by the way I was chewing. He could have spent the same time making money by drilling away and I would have 100% believed he was acting in my best interest. I was amazed at how well cared for I was by this

Chapter 3: Influential Characteristics

perfect stranger. As I made my copay, I asked the lady at the front desk about the doctor. Her reply was all I needed to hear: *That's just how he does business—we all love working with him and I won't work with anyone else.* His *habit* of fiduciary trust made his business flourish from his clients to his employees to the doctors who referred patients to him.

It's these types of professionals who realize that their greatest asset is the habitual fiduciary trust that others have in them, and who derive tremendous satisfaction from being trusted in that way. There is nothing mercenary about how they act. In professions in which the market is in play, they often do well financially, but they realize that money is simply a result—a lag measure—of trust. Trust is the lead measure of how well they do. If they cannot be habitually trusted to act in a fiduciary capacity, then ultimately they are commodities that can be dispensed with for cheaper options. But genuine peak influencers are disruption-proof: their expertise is backed and powered by the habitual fiduciary trust they inspire.

Fully Human

It's indisputable that there are myriad benefits that stem from a fundamentally deep trust. But there's one other that is worth mentioning that might trump all of the others. As far as I can tell, we become who we spend time with. For me, because I was spending time with people who habitually operated at this trust level, I actually became more and more trusted and as a result, became a better fiduciary and offered far better insights for my clients. There's something incredibly rewarding and deeply fulfilling about being trusted every hour you are working professionally. Anyone who has ever parented a teenager also knows what the rollercoaster of trust feels like when they start experimenting with keeping you at a distance and then letting you back in. You might say that we are designed to be trusted—that in living a life composed of delicate relationships, acquiring the profound trust of others resonates with us at the core of who we are as social beings. Whether at work or play, among family or strangers, to be trusted is to feel fully human.

Chapter 3: Influential Characteristics

The three forms of trust I encountered in people I met along my journey to build a business correlate with the three forms of longevity covered earlier in this chapter:

o At the bottom were people for whom the majority of their professional trust was "transactional"—merely sufficient for the here and now. As with longevity, most professions relied simply on this sort of trust.

o In the middle section were individuals for whom trust was a "bonus"—a nice added benefit to their clients, but not absolutely necessary to pay the bills.

o And at the top were the peak influencers for whom trust was "fundamental"—inseparable from their success.

TYPES OF TRUST ESTABLISHED

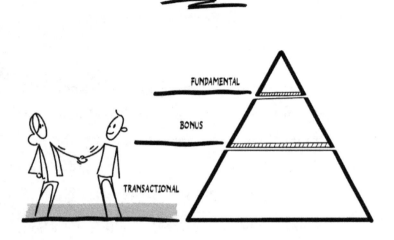

Trust's Transfer

When professionals embrace trust as fundamental to their worldview, take on the mantle of habitual fiduciary responsibility and forge a track record of trust with their clients, a powerful thing happens: they can transfer that trust to anyone they choose. It's transferred when an influencer tells a client, customer or constituent of any kind to contact her best agent, broker or attorney. It is

Chapter 3: Influential Characteristics

similarly transferred when you recommend a nursing home for a friend's aging mother. And habitual fiduciary qualities of trust are transferred as well when your family doctor recommends a psychologist who serves his own family or your pastor recommends a spiritual guide in the faraway town where you just got that new job.

Tellingly, just as was the case with longevity, if you want the trust of a peak influencer to transfer to you, the peak influencer has to see you as worthy of it. Trust is precious in large part because it takes time to win—and even then, it is viewed as fragile. Because trust is fragile, those who bear the honor of a habitual fiduciary trust are careful when entrusting their clients to a third party. To gain the trust of a peak influencer you need to be on your way to becoming one yourself. It's not enough to be simply trustworthy in transactional or bonus situations.

In my own business, I have found that the clients who are referred to me by peak influencers trust me implicitly from the word go. This is a fascinating reality in a world in which consumers are bombarded with calls to action and sales pitches. We all have our guard up and are reluctant to trust anyone lest we be the victim of an

Find Your Six

unscrupulous provider or even a scam. But the consumers I've had the luxury of dealing with as a result of influencers have very little of this hesitancy. And why would they hesitate? The recommendation they are acting on is from someone they have habitually come to trust as a fiduciary—someone who has acted in their best interest time and again.

The End of Trust?

You might think you are in a profession where your value doesn't actually hinge on trust. Take, for example, my field: with the dawn of the internet, many would argue that a real estate agent really doesn't need to be trusted anymore. Clients already have access to all of the listings online and all an agent really needs to do is open the door and prepare the paperwork. That view of my profession isn't wrong—for an increasing number of real estate agents, their value proposition revolves around little more than being a facilitator. As a consumer, there is not a perceived cost in switching one facilitator out for another. Facilitators are commodities, and when what

Chapter 3: Influential Characteristics

you do is commoditized, your value plummets, as all you have to compete on is price.

The same could be argued about attorneys, financial planners and pretty much every other service industry you can think of: attorneys who don't create enough value lose business to LegalZoom; financial planners to Schwab, etc.

But attorneys who are known for being great habitual fiduciaries, completely trustworthy in how they work and act, don't have any problem finding business and charging what they're worth. In fact, they can charge at the high end of the spectrum. The same is true for other businesses that rely on being peak influencers. The best thing about business referred to you by professionals who are trusted at the highest levels is that you almost never compete on price. They don't haggle with a professional who is referred to them by someone they trust implicitly. Because the peak influencer has transferred their trust, their clients trust that you will be worth every penny—and more.

Peak influencers, therefore, hold the keys to clients who trust you because of the trusting relationships in

Find Your Six

which they themselves are immersed. Growing your business means finding these influencers. Simple ideas need simple rules to be implemented, so I created a second rule for myself: ***look for those individuals who are at or above your trust level professionally.***

Characteristic 3: Caring About Outcomes

If longevity lays a foundation for trust, it then creates the conditions for the third and final characteristic that defines peak influencers: an owner's mindset. And just as the longevity and trust needed to be a peak influencer is different from that found in their run-of-the-mill counterparts, the same is doubly true when considering this third and arguably most important characteristic of peak influencers.

Now you probably think I'm not telling you anything new by saying if you can forge connections with owners of businesses you'll do well with your own. But let me be clear: that's *not* what I'm saying. In fact, there's a far cry between being an owner and having an ownership mentality.

Chapter 3: Influential Characteristics

There are many different ways to own a business. Some people inherit the business from their family and take a caretaker role, having not been on the ground floor when it was created. Others grow their businesses dramatically, but frankly flounder when it comes to being an owner of a scaled-up company. Still others confuse ownership with micro-managing, insisting that only with their input will anything succeed. These are all ways of owning a company, but that doesn't necessarily mean they will display an ownership mentality. Owners who don't have an ownership mentality fundamentally confuse running a business or managing a business with truly owning a business. Their name may be on the company door, but it doesn't mean they necessarily approach their work as an owner.

Having an ownership mentality is not just focusing on the day-to-day or week to week but thinking ahead in terms of months and years. It's being both the heartbeat of the organization and its visionary while inspiring colleagues to take more ownership of their roles. It's showing up each and every day energized by the challenge and opportunities that lie ahead. Those with an

Find Your Six

ownership mentality act in all these ways, and in the end that's what makes them peak influencers.

It's both easier and harder to approach the task of finding those peak influencers with an ownership mentality versus looking for owners. On the one hand, owners by definition are few and far between, whereas those in business who have an ownership mentality reside at all levels of companies. But on the other hand, while it's easy to identify the owners of a company, it's harder to suss out who truly has an ownership mentality.

9 to 5

Before my siblings and I were big enough to work for my dad's construction company on the weekends, Saturday mornings in our house often consisted of *Life* cereal and watching cartoons. We were not allowed to watch TV during the week, so our anticipation of the cartoons was admittedly illogically high. We would settle into our favorite spot on the couch and eagerly await our favorite cartoon—the Flintstones—and its iconic opening scene: Fred is dutifully riding a dinosaur at his construction site job when his boss pulls the tail of

Chapter 3: Influential Characteristics

a prehistoric bird who screeches, marking the end of the workday. Fred gleefully exclaims "Yabba-dabba-do!!"—work is over and life has begun.

Fred's relationship with his job can bubble up in all of us at the end of a long week. We can't wait to be finished and get on with the weekend, darting around in our prehistoric car ordering brontosaurus burgers with our friends. Even as a kid I could relate: after all, wasn't that how school felt as Friday afternoon rolled around? Why shouldn't work feel the same way?

For the majority of the people you know, work really does feel this way. The Freds of the world work for the weekend. They put their job behind them when they leave the office, shut off their computer or clock out. There's even a "West Coast" mantra that captures this attitude: "Work to live not live to work."

I want to be perfectly clear that there's nothing wrong with this attitude. The vast majority of workers adopt precisely this approach and this mentality does not prevent them from doing their work well. Many are quite excellent at what they do and even find great satisfaction and enjoyment in what they do (driving a dinosaur

Find Your Six

does look like fun!). But because they have a 9 to 5 mentality with respect to their work, they simply do not have an ownership mentality. In the search for peak influencers, those with a "work it" mentality can be crossed off the list.

Owners, Not Workaholics

Having an "ownership mentality" is not the opposite in hours on the job of a "work it" mentality. It does not mean being a workaholic. It's not about the number of hours you put in but an attitude you bring to your work. Those with an ownership mentality feel the pulse of a company and can speak knowledgeably about its health. They feel genuine joy with the growth of the company and suffer with every setback. Who they are is woven into the fabric of the organization such that when you know them, you know their business. It doesn't mean that they can't step back and enjoy their weekends. Indeed, because they know how to invest their time in what's valuable they squeeze the most joy out of their downtime as well. In short, someone with an ownership mentality is invested in the company in a

Chapter 3: Influential Characteristics

way that Fred just isn't. If you are an entrepreneur, a genuine owner or have a ton of independence in how you work, the feeling Fred has at the end of the week ought to be foreign to you.

Owning Adversity

It's not much of a challenge identifying the differences between those with a "work it" mindset and those with an ownership mentality. But finding peak influencers with an ownership mindset requires separating those with what I call a "run it" mindset from the true owners, and that turns out to be considerably harder to do. In fact, too often those who have a "run it" mindset in an organization can be mistaken for peak influencers. I know because it happened to me.

When I was starting my career, I was networking with a group of other young professionals. One of them was in the title business. He looked every bit the part of an owner to my inexperienced eyes at the time. He was very successful: he drove the car, wore the suits and even had the corner office to prove it. He was constantly on

Find Your Six

the move and had a command of his business that I found impressive. He even sent me some business and I made sure to send him a lot of mine. Our professional relationship seemed strong.

Then the market took a historically bad turn. At the time, I was involved in a deal in which he was selling an investment property. The day before we settled he ordered me to pay the buyer's agent less than what we had promised since his margins were no longer within the amount he had budgeted. When I told him that we could not legally do this, he sulked away cursing. Within the week he was nowhere to be found. One of his colleagues told me that he simply packed up his desk and walked out, leaving the company in the lurch. It turns out several other deals he had in the works were only going to produce the thinnest of margins for him, and rather than face the consequences he just quit the field of play. The owner I thought I knew turned out to be somebody else entirely. When things were good, he could run his business with all of the external trappings of an owner, but when adversity hit—as it inevitably does—he abandoned ship.

Chapter 3: Influential Characteristics

This experience changed forever who I would link my professional reputation to and illustrates a key distinguishing feature between those with a "run it" mindset and those with an ownership mentality: when push comes to shove, how do they react? Are they willing to take responsibility or do they blame and make excuses? Will they "own it" when things are hard or will they fold their tent?

Now to be sure I don't want to suggest that everyone with a "run it" approach to a job is liable to flake out at the smallest sign of adversity. Nor am I suggesting that the only way to find out if you're dealing with someone with an ownership mentality is to experience a crisis like I did. But what I am saying is that those with an owner mindset *embrace* the burden of acquiring business, driving revenue or donations, and increasing the customer base while building referral relationships. They don't just execute on the business, managing expenses and updating systems. Instead, responsibility for the outcomes of the business is something for which they take full responsibility and they immerse themselves in the game of influencing these outcomes. Like any good player in a game, their sporting spirit drives them and makes the game something they can't imagine clocking out of. It's not a role they take on and can just as easily take off. Their identity is wrapped up in their influence on the game. If anyone can ever be called indispensable to the organization, it is those who possess the "own it" mindset.

Who's in Charge Here?

One challenge with defining roles within organizations is that they pigeon-hole someone's ability to play the game. For example, many organizations have roles that are either responsible for "revenue funnel" activities—pure salespeople—or roles for those who are completely consumed with internal execution and have little direct influence on revenue coming in the door— pure administrators. Fred's role was to drive that dinosaur all day long. The role of his boss was to make sure Fred and his fellow employees gave him a full day's labor.

Even when titles seem to pigeonhole people (Executive Assistant, Director of Operations, Vice President . . .), those who truly have an "own it"

Chapter 3: Influential Characteristics

approach are not limited by these boundaries. Instead of being concerned with a transaction of their time for money, they are concerned with outcomes. Unsurprisingly, many people who actually own companies have an owner mindset, particularly the ones who are very successful. But as we've seen, there are some people at the "top" of organizations who are checked out of the game. They are on the field physically, but their sporting spirit is nowhere to be found. They are just running or managing companies, not leading them. I can't stress this enough: management is not the same as the total ownership mindset necessary to invest in employees such that a real impact or influence can be had. Owners who manage instead of "own it" often reap the rewards of profits in the short term, but they don't have the skin in the game that the owner mindset requires. If the ship goes down, they will be disappointed, but they are not going down with it.

Conversely, as in the case of longevity and trust, the ownership mindset can and does exist in the ranks of people who are not technically the owners of the firm. There are secretaries, HR directors, janitors and even

Find Your Six

people with managerial titles who in fact lead and influence because of their "own it" mindset. In fact, in healthy businesses, an ownership mindset can be found at every level of the organization, from the lowest-paid staffer to the most senior partner.

Just as was the case with longevity and trust, it seems that there are three different kinds of mindsets in business, which we can apply to our pyramid layers:

o At the bottom are the majority of workers who put in a good day's work and clock out at the end of the day. While many are excellent at what they do, they have no inherent interest in the business beyond a steady paycheck.

o In the middle of the pyramid are those individuals who manage or run the business. They oftentimes appear to have ownership-level influence but ultimately are more interested in moving the pieces on the board versus causing the game to happen in the first place.

Chapter 3: Influential Characteristics

o And then there are those with an ownership mentality at the top of the pyramid. These peak influencers are intertwined with their work. Their success is inseparable from the business' success.

Find Your Six

The Insights of Ownership

What do true owners know (regardless of their title) that those with a "run it" or a "work it" approach don't? They know that for their firms to grow and flourish they have to connect with other owners. It's not just a matter of efficiency, though that certainly is a part of the calculation that owners make. It's understanding that when you connect with another with an owner's mentality—whether their name is on the building or they are in a delivery truck—you have found a resource who can open doors you could rarely anticipate. Sometimes the door is information that is critical to your business. Sometimes the door is a system or process that makes your business more reliant or profitable. And sometimes that door leads to additional doors being opened for you since you're now part of that other peak influencer's network. As was the case with longevity and trust, this fluid transfer of resources is invaluable. It's all because those with an "own it" mindset recognize and value others who "own it."

Chapter 3: Influential Characteristics

When owners put their name to yours, transferring their reputation and trust to you, the client is not a lead but rather a relationship that has been entrusted to you. The same is true when an influencer sends you a candidate for a role in your organization, or when they connect you to a colleague they think will benefit you. Owners are in the business of influence, and if you can help them in this mission, they will see you as an asset. That's not to say that getting others with an ownership mentality to open the door will be easy. There are no shortcuts when it comes to convincing someone with an ownership mentality to welcome you in. They are hard to win over, but once they are on your team, they are faithful advocates for your business.

It's well worth your while, then, to seek these peak influencers out and make the connection. There's plenty to say about how to make that connection—the rest of this book is, in fact, all about that. But there's one thing that has to happen first before you can even contemplate making such a connection. You have to fully embrace an ownership mentality yourself.

Find Your Six

Cultivating **Your** Ownership Mentality

By now it should come as no surprise why your success hinges on acquiring an ownership mentality. Those with an ownership mentality only want to deal with other individuals who share their outlook. After all, this is a reciprocal relationship: even if you don't have goods or services that they need, they probably know someone who does need what you can offer, and you're valuable to them if you can help the other owners in their network with whom they already do business. But they're not going to recommend you to those in their network if you can't deliver on what you say you can. And who is the kind of person who can deliver regardless of obstacles or roadblocks, who never makes excuses and is always up to the challenge? Someone with an ownership mentality themselves.

Let's be honest: pre-2008 when the real estate market was going great guns, everyone in my office was selling homes left and right. I got into the business at a time that was perfect for learning the ropes and experiencing what I thought was some early success. But what I discovered

Chapter 3: Influential Characteristics

is that truly successful businesses don't just survive downturns—they find ways to flourish during them as well. It's not enough to work at it or even to manage your business to grow it even during lean years—you really have to be an owner if you're going to succeed.

Those in business with a real ownership mindset know this. They're truly not interested in flash in the pan successes, because those successes burn brightly—but burn out just as fast. They're only interested in those individuals like themselves who are built for the long haul—who have an ownership mindset that will ensure that they do not just stay afloat and weather the storm but in fact can still navigate during high seas and tumultuous conditions. It's these individuals and businesses you can count on to deliver. They stand the test of time and are trusted because they are guided by individuals with an ownership mentality.

Genuine owners are peak influencers because they have a nose for other owners. If you want to find them, start by becoming one yourself, because the long-term survival of your business will depend on it. Not only will your firm benefit by your steady hand on the rudder, but

Find Your Six

you'll have plenty of lighthouses and tugboats—guidance, support and business from your fellow owners—when (not if) the storm comes. My rule when it comes to owners is simply this: ***true owners only do business with other professionals who have skin in the game.***

Conclusion

At some point in our lives most of us will need to get glasses. For me, this happened about ten years ago. Like most people who don glasses for the first time, I was amazed by the details I could see with ease. The glasses crystalized everything. I was less fatigued when reading and, according to my kids, they even made me look smarter.

At this point, you should have the image of the pyramid forming in your mind's eye such that you can begin applying the pyramid to your relationships for your business. Like a new pair of glasses, the pyramid will become a prism through which you will be able to see with crystal clarity. At the bottom of your pyramid, you'll

Chapter 3: Influential Characteristics

see the short-term, transactional, "work it" types. In the middle will come into view many of the service professionals who spend about a week or less of time with their clients, for whom trust is often just an added bonus, and who take a decidedly managerial, "run it" approach to their profession. And at the very top of the pyramid, you'll focus in on a sliver of genuine influencers. These are the professionals who clock the most time with their clients, constituents and coworkers, the ones who make up the DNA of the company and who are trusted implicitly because they approach even the most seemingly insignificant aspects of their work with a mindset of complete ownership.

PART II
FINDING INFLUENCE

Each year I have the distinct honor of working with five young professionals who are embarking on their careers through a program I helped cofound called the DC Accelerator. It's an absolute blast to help guide these young, bright minds in their eagerness to take on the world. They all come from different backgrounds, have different interests and are each motivated in unique ways. But sadly, when they come into the program, they almost all have one thing in common: few, if any of them, have deep relationships with mentors. While they may have encountered a good teacher or perhaps brushed past an enthusiastic coach in high school, as they channel their energy to launching into professional life, they don't know where to turn. Two things have become clear to me and the team at the DC Accelerator over the years. First, that the brightest professionals with the best ideas

Find Your Six

and sharpest curriculum vitae will not have the success they could without a way of thinking that comes of a deep connection with an invested mentor, someone to help guide their strong base of knowledge into uniquely superb, wise insights. And second, that when these same insights are not present for business owners, no matter their drive, market position or the quality of product or service they have, they tend to fail. Who we surround ourselves with has a profound impact on our lives. This fundamental truth is at the root of the need to find influencers as you build your business.

At this point, you should have a really clear picture of the cost to your business of not finding influencers. You should also understand what makes someone a true influencer for you and your business. But if you're like me, you're hungry for a road map: the tactics that you can use every day to set meetings, have great conversations and continue to invest in the most likely candidates. That's what we'll uncover in the rest of this book.

Chapter 4

LANDING INFLUENCER CANDIDATE MEETINGS

"We're paying the highest tribute you can pay a man. We trust him to do right. It's that simple."

HARPER LEE
TO KILL A MOCKINGBIRD

All journeys have a beginning. It's at the beginning where the single most crucial decision is made, the decision to cast off despite not knowing what you will encounter. Every journey requires some leap of faith.

Find Your Six

And because of this requirement, most failure happens right at the beginning.

You may remember driving in an age before GPS when all we had were paper roadmaps. These were helpful but not foolproof, and it was easy to get disoriented and end up going the wrong way. Some of us were more stubborn than others. "I've got a good sense of direction," I would say. Others (like my wife) would have enough sense to pull over at a gas station or a shop or they would wave to another driver at a stoplight and **ask for directions.**

To begin your influencer journey requires you to make an ask of somebody. If you've read this far you know what—or rather *who*—you are looking for. Your destination is clear. But the route to them can't be found on Google Maps. *You're going to have to ask for directions.* I can give you clarity on the coordinates, but the turns in the roads will need to be navigated by asking the locals.

Landing meetings with influencers is as basic as asking for directions. It's a simple but sincere request, as I'll explain below in some detail. If you can't ask for that, nobody's going to show you the way to your destination.

Chapter 4: Landing Influencer Candidate Meetings

If so much can be achieved by pulling over to ask for directions, why don't we do it? Is it because we want to believe we know the way already? Is it because we don't want anyone to see that we have not yet "made it?" Is it because our ego gets in the way? Is it that we were never taught how to ask for directions? The answer to all these questions is yes. Your fears are *true*.

Yes: you don't know the way already. Yes: you've not made it yet and the person you're asking will know this. Yes: your ego is preventing you from admitting this. And yes: your training to this point has likely never taught you how to ask for directions or who to flag down to ask for directions.

You need to first conquer your fears before you can ask for directions the right way. So let's start there.

Eating your Ego

In the framework that I'm offering to you in this book, asking for directions is as simple and as difficult as asking for a meeting with someone who might be an influencer. And ego often gets in the way.

There's a little voice in your head that says:

97

Find Your Six

"What if they say 'no'?"

"What if no one wants to meet with me?"

"What if I spend all this money and time on coffee only to find out that people don't like me?"

And then, in a moment of extreme cowardice, the voice turns on you completely:

"Gee… maybe paying for those (admittedly crappy) online leads really *is* my path to incredible wealth and success after all."

Bam: you're derailed. You've stopped thinking like an influencer and gone back to thinking like a dung-shoveler. And all you had to do was pick up the phone and ask for a meeting. You didn't have to learn a script, handle objections, or come up with a special money-back guarantee. All you had to do was ask for directions.

To be clear: if you can overcome your fears and ask for directions, you *will* arrive at your destination—much faster, in fact, than had you just kept driving without a clue as to where you were headed. There will be very few wrong turns as a result, and in the process you'll find guides along your path you would have never encountered if your ego had its way. It's the difference

Chapter 4: Landing Influencer Candidate Meetings

between wandering in the desert for 40 years or gaining sight of the promised land in six months—and it all depends on what you do at this critical first step.

Let me make it even easier for you by helping you make the list of who you're going to ask.

Where to Start: Friends and Neighbors

Like a lot of major cities, the Washington DC area has a highway system known as the beltway that encircles the entire city. When folks are new to the region they can easily end up going the wrong way on this massive loop. You want to feel like you have control and know where you are going; you are the one driving after all! But before you know it, if you didn't ask for directions right at the start, something will just feel off about the direction you are headed and you'll find yourself mumbling under your breath, "Are you sure this is the right way?"

Where do you begin your journey of getting directions for finding your influencers? With the people closest to you—your current sphere of influence. The

Find Your Six

people you can see from your driveway before you even start driving. Begin with friends, neighbors and business owners you know today. If you ask for help at the beginning of your journey, you will set off in the right direction. At the beginning Frodo had Gandalf. Luke had Obi-Wan. Start with the ones who are right next to you.

Since everything hinges on making your first asks of people you know today, your first task is to make a list of everyone you know. Everyone you are connected to on social media, everyone you went to school with, your parents' friends, the people from the chamber of commerce, from past jobs, from church, your kid's soccer team, and the community pool. Don't worry about what they do or where you think they are on the pyramid. Leave no stone unturned. Just make the *longest* list possible.

Once you have that list, ask yourself: from which of these people would I most like to learn something? Give some thought to each name. If you believe they might be able to offer some particular insight, write that down next to their name. If you are not sure what the insight would be but have a sense that with a little research you

Chapter 4: Landing Influencer Candidate Meetings

would find them more intriguing to speak with than most, make a note to do that research. Just identify those on the list who could *offer you advice.*

Admittedly, what your friends are probably expecting to hear when you approach them is something akin to a pitch. Something canned. Something that sounds like the following: "If you or someone you know were looking for [insert service or product such as a new home, life insurance, a comprehensive financial plan, help drafting a will, etc. . . .] would you consider using me?"

This is precisely what you should not do. What you will ask of them instead is to think of you in an entirely different way.

And when you cause those who know you today to think of you differently, they will look *forward* to the opportunity to connect you with their friends, colleagues and people who trust them. They will open the door to the treasure trove of their network for you. They will grow your list for you. When people are willing to associate their reputation with yours and connect you to the people with whom they have built trust, the new relationship starts on a firm footing with fantastic energy

101

that you just can't get by meeting people at a networking meeting.

And guess what? If you invest in your new connections correctly, they will also eagerly connect you to their networks. And so it goes.

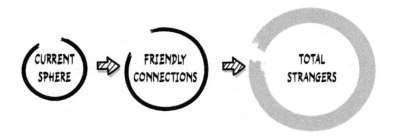

This may seem incredibly simplistic, but there's really no reason to overcomplicate the matter. At their core, influencers are people to whom others routinely look for advice. At this stage of the journey, if you believe someone is worth chatting with over coffee to gain some insight, advice or wise counsel, chances are others feel the same way. That's the simple truth of how to embark on narrowing down your list to your first group of influencer candidates.

Chapter 4: Landing Influencer Candidate Meetings

Starting (not Ending) in Place

Let's understand something right at the outset: the people you know today are not going to be the people who directly help you build your next great business. They won't typically be your influencers. However, the people you know today almost certainly will be the people who give you the right early directions on your journey to find your influencers.

That's right: your best influencers are likely not the ones you know today. In fact, on my team, we have an adage: "99 of the 100 people you know today are not the people who will build wealth for you tomorrow." It's an intentionally extreme reminder that you have to constantly be in a talent search mode unless you want to have a disruption-prone business. How many good professionals aggressively pursue relationships early in their career? When their hard work pays off, they land a major account or two at an established company, but as their career progresses, they become far less intentional about investing into these relationships. Suddenly the market shifts, their long-time advocate in the company

Find Your Six

opts for early retirement, and the funnel of business abruptly turns off. Had they been in talent search mode as a matter of habit, their business would have dealt with the loss as a simple bump in the road. But without internalizing this truth about the talent they know today, the bump turns into a catastrophic sinkhole. You can't rely on the same people to build your business in year five as built your business in year one.

Similarly, when you are just getting started in the business, you can't rely on the people you knew before you got into the business to make you successful. If you want to build a disruption-proof business, it's the talented people you will meet by implementing this framework who will see you as a professional they want to grow alongside. I personally learned this the hard way.

Like many people, I built a business in the same town that I grew up in. But it wasn't my close friends and family who helped me grow my company exponentially. They loved me, they were excited for me and were some of my biggest cheerleaders. I would even get an occasional referral from them—but they were not the ones who drove significant revenue for my business. Had I relied

104

Chapter 4: Landing Influencer Candidate Meetings

on referrals from family and friends alone, I would never have provided for my family, built a company, and certainly not achieved any degree of financial freedom. Instead, it was the people I met systematically through this process who really moved the needle for me. People I didn't know at the beginning of my career were the people who kept revenue coming in years two and three and beyond.

People often ask me, "If I don't know anyone in a completely new town, where do I start?" My answer is that this is your home town now, so you start in the same place you would if you had lived there all your life: chambers, volunteer opportunities, political campaigns, church, school, sports teams, and even the gym. Be a magnet for making friends. Take interest in people, what they do for a living, how they think, and they will be happy to grab a cup of coffee with you. All you need is a genuine spirit of curiosity in others.

In some ways, there is an advantage to being in an entirely different land than the one where everyone knows you from your previous life or profession. You're starting from scratch. It's like going to college out of town. It's your opportunity to define who you are to people who don't have any preconceived idea of what you can offer them. You've got a blank slate.

You are also free from the expectation that the people you've known all your life are going to choose you simply because they know you and trust you in other realms outside of your professional life. Even today, when someone who has known me all my life doesn't use my company to buy or sell, it's a punch in the gut. The only way to feel alright about this is to have more business predictably coming in the door.

The Three Categories of Acceptable Asks

Landing meetings with influencer candidates is both the simplest idea in this book and where most people will fail. They will fail because they don't know *how* to ask for the meeting. And there's a sad reason for this. They have been trained to think that what they should be doing is pitching business, which means they won't be able to make a truly sincere ask. They should be asking for advice and insight, but they just can't help themselves. It's

Chapter 4: Landing Influencer Candidate Meetings

as though they think they have only two options: keep driving as fast as possible without asking for directions, hoping they are headed in the right direction, or stop and tell the person they would otherwise ask for directions where they think they are going since they are so convinced that the direction they are headed in must be the right way. This seems absurd, but it's precisely what happens when we pitch someone, trying to make a quota and allowing short-term goals to direct our activities. In so doing we can miss out on what could be won by actually asking and allowing someone to guide our path.

Think about it from the perspective of the person you're supposed to be asking for advice but instead are not-so-secretly pitching. What you are doing is attempting to cause the person to feel like *they* are the ones that need help (in the form of your service) instead of the other way round. And while an influencer is always on the prowl for opportunities to grow their own business, they didn't get to where they are listening to cold pitches. After all, if they needed assistance, wouldn't they turn to their incredible network first and foremost?

Find Your Six

I can guarantee one certain outcome if you go about the ask the wrong way: if you make a pitch, you will not get the meeting. But on the flip side, there are three categories of asks that will — without fail — open up meeting after meeting for you. They work because they are authentic — an ask that is utterly sincere because it is *just* an ask.

Ask #1: Ask for Advice

Have you ever had someone ask you for advice? Sure you have.

Did you get mad at them for asking you for your advice? If you're normal, you didn't get mad at all. Instead, you likely felt honored and special. It's a sign of recognition to have someone ask for your advice. To be asked for advice is a gift: someone just gave you a great compliment!

As the asker, if you learn the craft of how to ask for advice authentically, humbly, and with a real interest in the advice that you are seeking, you will almost never get rejected. No matter how old you are or experienced you are in your business, if you learn this little skill you can

Chapter 4: Landing Influencer Candidate Meetings

build an amazing business and hang out with some phenomenal people along the way.

When I was new in the business, asking for advice was incredibly easy. I would say something to the effect of, "I've really admired what I know of your business and career and, as you may know, I'm just starting mine. If you could find the time, I'd love to understand what has gone into building such a successful business for you. Would you be up for a cup of coffee in the next week or so? I'm happy to come to you at whatever time is most convenient for your schedule."

You can imagine that there are a lot of iterations on this basic idea. If you want to be sure never to come across as scripted, you will need to cater your conversation to the specific person. It shouldn't be scripted at all. For example, let's imagine you are trying to get a meeting on the calendar with someone who travels a good deal. You might say something like, "I was meeting with Angela just the other day and she spoke very highly of how you have balanced your personal life with traveling and managing your people. I'm working to take my business to a new level and would love to chat with you about how you've achieved this. I know you're very busy, but would you ever be up for a coffee or an early breakfast? Since I know you do a lot of traveling, I'd be more than happy to meet you at the airport if that works best for your schedule."

There are a few things going on in this request to meet:

- *Mutuality*: You are referencing your mutual contact and that she was willing to meet with you. If Angela spent her valuable time with you, her contact will be more open to a meeting.

- *Respect*: You are referring to how Angela respects this person. This is not flattery so much as a non-generic nod to why you are making the ask. You are not saying "random people say great things about you." Instead, it's that Anegla—someone they know and respect too—is the conduit because of her respect for you.

- *Specific Framing*: You don't just ask to pick the person's brain about whatever the heck comes up

Chapter 4: Landing Influencer Candidate Meetings

over coffee. They know that you are interested in speaking about business and that you would like their professional advice. You've framed your reason for the conversation. Framing this way shows authentic purpose and intentionality— which is exactly what a salesperson with a pitch will want to hide since their entire intention is to sell.

o **Convenience**: You respect the fact that they have a lot of demands pulling on them and make your request for their time as easy as possible. Your offer implies that it's so important to meet that you will be happily inconvenienced if that means you can have the benefit of their insights.

A request to meet that has these elements is nearly failproof. I say nearly because I'm sure there are some circumstances in which someone could get a rejection. But I've never been rejected when these elements are in place. I mean, would you ever say no to this request?

These elements are only enhanced when Angela doesn't just give you permission to use her name but

Find Your Six

actually puts her name next to yours in an email, text or even a call. She warms up the referral and makes your four elements virtually impossible to ignore.

Ask #2: Ask for a Particular Insight

Another fantastic way to land a meeting is to ask for specific insights. These might include insights into a presentation you need to make, strategic plans you have for the business, or new frameworks through which to guide clients. For me, these were often client presentations, whether for investors, builders or a specific type of buyer or seller. They might also include a new product line or variation. You might ask about best hiring practices that the candidate uses in a situation in which you are preparing to bring on staff.

These are fantastic conversations for two important reasons. The first reason is because its specificity means it is authentic. When someone requests counsel from you in an area in which you are particularly gifted, it shows the person is serious about the conversation and has done the homework on you. Using the example of

Chapter 4: Landing Influencer Candidate Meetings

the seller presentation I mentioned, here's what this request for a meeting might sound like:

"In dealing with your accounts in the tech world, I know you have to be very sharp in how you present ideas and show your value against your competition. I've been creating a presentation for my prospective sellers that I think will move my close ratio up significantly, but I'd really like to get your professional take on it. Frankly, I need someone who presents at a high level to beat me up on my presentation. Would you be open to grabbing a coffee to allow me a chance to get your insights?"

Here again you can see how specificity is endearing. Getting presentations or new product lines vetted this way is immensely valuable in itself for the refinement of the presentation. It also gives them permission to be open and honest with you, allowing them not to pull their punches if they see something that just doesn't gel. And its frankness can cause them to become an advocate as they learn more about how you think and what you do.

Of course, the way this approach can go sideways is if you start pitching the product to the influencer. As soon as you shift from collaborating on how to better the

Find Your Six

pitch to asking if they want what you are selling, you lose them. These are smart, insightful people. You can't fool them. If they want what you have, they will ask for it—and sometimes they will. But your goal here is not to get their business but to stay focused on future business: both by improving your presentation and by letting this highly connected influencer know that this is what you sell. After all, what's better in the end: getting their individual business or getting the business of several other influences within their circle of influence?

The second reason why this kind of ask is so effective is that "it's business, not buddies." When your ask is focused on business, there's no question that you are a professional. And you can't afford to be thought of by the candidate as anything but a serious professional. Influencers put their professional reputation behind great businesses and the professionals who drive the success of the business. They don't put their reputation behind people they just enjoy having coffee with.

The final reason the particular insight approach works is that it focuses on the language of business. People at the top of the pyramid speak the language of business no

Chapter 4: Landing Influencer Candidate Meetings

matter what field they are in—college professors, non-profits or retail shop owners. When you show that you speak like a business owner, when your interests lie in the concerns that owners have every day, influencers will see you as a peer even if you have yet to realize many of the major accomplishments that they have had.

But what if they are busy? That's a good sign, of course—they're probably not an influencer if they have time on their hands to see you later in the day or tomorrow. They may not have time to offer you their advice at the moment, but if time is taken off the table, they'd be happy to meet with anyone who is humble enough to ask for a specific insight. If the ask is authentic, they'll find the time to meet even if the meeting gets pushed out a month or even two.

Find Your Six

Influencer Profile: Ben Landers

I met Ben Landers when Rich, an influencer who has also become a great personal friend and consistent referral source, introduced us. Ben runs an extremely successful national marketing company. As soon as I met Ben I knew he had the potential to be hugely influential for my business. I had to resist the urge to sell him on me, but boy I'm glad I did. I can think of at least four great pieces of business advice that Ben has given me over the years, crucial stuff that allowed me to run a better operation: sales and marketing advice, hiring advice, even advice on leasing property. Ben has also recommended a number of fantastic business books over the years. With each book, Ben has not just answered a specific question but opened up new horizons for my business. Many of these books have made it into my personal top 20 that I recommend to others. The wealth of advice, insight, connections and, yes, referrals from Ben has been massively impactful for me. The bond we have forged really moved the needle for my company.

Is there any way I don't think of Ben when I hear of someone in the trades needing marketing help? And is

Chapter 4: Landing Influencer Candidate Meetings

there any way I don't think of Rich when Ben invests in me?

Not a chance.

What's even more striking is that I've run into many other people Ben knows who have benefited in a similar way as I have from their relationship with Ben. They have kids on the same swim team as Ben, live on the same street as Ben, or go to the same church as Ben. Ben is always deploying his business sense for others in a completely natural and generous way.

Here's another fact: Ben's company made the Inc. 5000 list of the fastest-growing privately held companies for eight years in a row. Coincidence?

Not a chance.

Ask #3: Ask How You Can Help Them

The final acceptable ask is one in which you are primarily concerned with helping them. It sets up a meeting during which you are influencing the influencer as much as or more than they are influencing you. This type of meeting will only happen when you truly have

Find Your Six

something to offer the influencer candidate that you know can impact them.

Hearing about this option you may say to yourself, "This is great! I have a product or service that I believe everyone needs! My meetings can be both helpful to the influencer <u>and</u> a sales call!" But, as should be clear by now, this would in fact be the greatest killer of influencer relationships.

Instead of a veiled sales call, these are conversations in which you lay down your immediate desire to sell and focus entirely on the goal of helping an influencer achieve what he or she is after. These are the hardest type of meetings to pull off early in your career, but eventually—as you gain influence in your own right and build authentic, trusting relationships—this type of ask for a meeting can and should become the heartbeat of your business.

Imagine a candidate list where instead of asking the question I suggested for building your initial list, "*What do I want to learn from this influential person?*" you asked instead, "*How can I truly help this influential person?*" The answer to this question is gold, but gold is not mined

Chapter 4: Landing Influencer Candidate Meetings

easily. This is why this type of meeting is often a second or third meeting with the influencer. These meetings will likely be separated by months and the earlier meetings will need to have been conducted by you in such a way that you now know what it is you can do to help them. You've arrived at the source of the gold and now are ready to give it away.

This call, email or even a text may go something like this:

"Hey Angela, I've been mulling over what you mentioned about looking for a new assistant and how you are concerned about making the wrong hire. We just brought on someone and used a new onboarding process that absolutely blew me away. We definitely made a better hire than I would have ever expected. I'd be thrilled to walk you through it if you'd like. I'll be down near your office at the end of the week and could do coffee or an early breakfast on Friday if that works for you."

Again, this works because of the same criteria we've noted above: The **language of business** is present and the **specificity** proves the ask is authentic, your **mutuality** has already been established and is fortified because of a mutual problem that you can solve, and you are making it as **convenient** as possible to meet. Added to this is the fact that you are expressing a true concern for Angela. Is there any wonder whether you will strike gold?

Will the payback happen at the meeting? Probably not. But if you've correctly identified that Angela is an influencer instead of just a leech, you can be certain that she'll have her ear to the ground for ways she could wind up helping you.

The other way these meetings will happen for you is through influencers who see your value and want their people to benefit from you. Instead of you doing the asking, you will become an influencer for others. What kind of business would you have if every day, because of the reputation you have as an influencer, you were asked to invest into others?

Eat your heart out lead gen.

Asks That Fall Short

Speaking of cheap substitutes for real relationships, trust, and influence, just as there are acceptable asks, there are three things that you absolutely, positively need

Chapter 4: Landing Influencer Candidate Meetings

to avoid when making the ask. These are not just types of requests that get ignored but that garner you ill will. If you don't believe me, just put yourself in the position of the person receiving one of these kinds of requests and see how you would react:

- o ***Presumption***: A request that is guaranteed to fail is one that assumes that the person on the receiving end has all the time in the world. I recently had someone ask over email to meet to talk about his business idea and he suggested that we should have two or three meetings about it. I responded that I'd be very happy to have a telephone call with him at first to find out more about what he's trying to do. I never heard back, which is just fine by me. But if I ever run into him again in person or just hear his name in passing … well, the request made an impression, and it wasn't a positive one.

- o ***Too general***: Another request that is guaranteed to fail is one where you have not done your homework to know how the person you're asking might be able to benefit from the conversation with you. You might permit this if they have been connected to you by an influencer, but if you were on the receiving end of a call that comes out of the blue or from a weak referral, *and* there is not a specific reason why the person asking wants to meet, would you justify spending valuable time with them that could otherwise be dedicated to important work or time with your loved ones?

o **The cold pitch**: Though I touched on this above, it can't be overstated: an ask where you are pitching an idea, especially when you've never met the person and they don't even know who you are yet, will derail any hope of setting the relationship off on the right foot. This is the equivalent of a cold call, and you will be viewed as a lead generator and not a potential influencer.

Conclusion

All great art stems from great preparation. The craft of making an effective ask is just as much something to

Chapter 4: Landing Influencer Candidate Meetings

master as the meeting itself. In fact, it's essential: who you need to speak to and why they are potentially influential is the canvas on which you'll paint your story and discover your influencers. The interplay of mutuality, respect, framing and convenience are the oil paints that you will mix, but without a canvas you'll be stuck fingerpainting. Be sure to invest the time and energy into landing the meeting the right way.

Chapter 5

THE ART OF THE MEETING

"Let us therefore animate and encourage each other, and show the whole world that a Freeman, contending for liberty on his own ground, is superior to any slavish mercenary on earth."

GEORGE WASHINGTON

You've done it—you've landed your appointment. That's the good news. Here's the bad news: You can set a lot of appointments and still squander the time... and most people do. This chapter is dedicated to

Find Your Six

making your meetings foolproof opportunities for connecting.

Since your objective is to find great talent, you need an approach to your meetings that allows you to see with clarity if you are sitting with talent that will end up at the top of your Influencer Pyramid. Your business depends on it. Every candidate you sit down with has the *potential* to be a peak influencer, but only a few will ultimately be a match for you. It is the art of the conversation you have at your meetings that will help you discover your peak influencer talent. Artists develop their skills inside of a framework or method. Your meetings will be exponenttially more productive if you too use a framework and adopt a methodology for conversing.

The difference between a meeting that is artfully conducted and one that isn't is similar to the difference between dancing with someone who leads well and dancing with someone who (while excited to dance) ends up stepping on your feet. It's an exhausting and frustrating way to pass time together, even if both parties can laugh it off down the road. But the truth is that even if influencers can chalk up your bad dancing to earnest

Chapter 5: The Art of the Meeting

clumsiness, they still won't want to go dancing again (and worse yet, they won't invite you to dance with others in their circle of influence). Best then to lead the dance artfully and find the talent you want to be in business with.

Whether it's salsa, swing, or hip hop, if you've ever been out dancing and you know how to lead a particular dance, you can quickly identify if your partner can follow. You know what to look for: it just feels right. If they are clumsy or have a different style that does not work with yours, you'll size it up quickly. There's either chemistry and a fit or there's not. Similarly, when you know what to look for, the art of your conversations will unveil the right partnerships, revealing whether your partner can cut a rug with you in the lead.

Doing your Homework

Have you ever had a meeting with someone who clearly didn't know exactly why you were meeting?

Maybe it was a doctor who had been booked solid for several hours before your appointment. You haven't seen

Find Your Six

him in a while, maybe years. He starts off needing an orientation before he can ask you any questions that get to the heart of why you are sitting on that table with the crinkly paper. The conversation suddenly feels far more transactional than you would like.

Regardless of the excuses around his lack of awareness—even perfectly legitimate excuses—you're probably not likely to recommend that doctor to your friends and family. But if the same doctor under the same set of circumstances had done a little homework, perhaps read your chart and spoken briefly with the nurse about her recollections of you, your impression could be very different. It's warmer.

When you meet with someone and you haven't done your homework, when you don't know where you want to take the conversation, you're digging out of a hole you didn't need to be in. Despite your best intentions, you can't lead the dance. There's no art to be made here.

Homework doesn't take long, but it does require that you sit down and do it. It adds color to the column of your initial list of candidates that answered the question of what you would like to learn from them (the first and

Chapter 5: The Art of the Meeting

most important background question being, "What am I interested in that they can teach me?"). Here are ten topic areas around their professional and personal lives you can focus on that will warm up your meeting and help you avoid coming off as a salesperson—thereby ruining your opportunity to make art of your meeting.

Professional Topic Areas

- o What do others say about them? Who do they surround themselves with?

- o How long have they been in their field or owned their company?

- o Where is their business going? How is their industry changing?

- o What is their company culture? Who do they hire as a result?

- o What do they like to talk about, read, or focus on in business?

Personal Topic Areas

- o Who is important to them?

Find Your Six

- How is their character reflected in their personal relationships?

- Who are you connected to in common on a personal level?

- What do they spend time doing outside of work?

- What is their sense of humor like?

I like doing this homework in a sprint format. You can find the answer to the majority of these questions in about 15 minutes (it's important <u>not</u> to spend an hour on this activity). People's profiles online reveal a lot. From there, you can find articles written, awards given, recommendations from colleagues. A simple Google search will turn up the good, the bad and the ugly about pretty much anyone.

The goal here is to know your subject such that you are able to be authentically interested in them and to ask great questions (not these questions, but questions based on your homework). Just like the doctor who is briefed

Chapter 5: The Art of the Meeting

on the next patient, your candidates will feel your authentic interest and respond accordingly.

When you do your homework, the result of your work should be a list of between three to five topics that you want to know more about. Fashioning questions out of them shows your clear human curiosity in the person you are talking to. The better your questions, the more likely your guest will lean back in the chair and figuratively (if not actually) say: "Wow—I love how this person thinks!"

The Reason You're Here

Put yourself in the shoes of the candidate invited to coffee. Let's assume that you've had a crazy morning of calls, appointments, and emails to respond to and perhaps even some personal issues to deal with. By the time 3:30 PM rolls around and you are sitting down for coffee, there's a decent chance that you are at least a bit foggy on the reason for your meeting. To boot, the appointment may have been booked a week or two ago. Anyone's brain can feel as if it's been to the moon and

Find Your Six

back in that timeframe. It's easy for even the best of professionals to have a lapse in focus. They are human, after all.

This is why it's imperative for you to set the stage for your conversation when you sit down at your meeting. Influencers, like the rest of the world, respond to the gift of clarity. Clarity is something that great leaders habitually provide and it's just good etiquette when meeting with someone. You are the host, and hosts have an obligation to their guests to set them at ease.

There's really nothing more derailing to what could be a dynamic conversation than enduring 15 minutes of small talk. Worse still is a meeting that begins with small talk complaining: "Do you believe this rain? ... Gosh I've been so slammed at work this week! ... Do you have teenagers ... ?" On the flip side, there's nothing that says "I honor your time" more than a warm welcome followed by clarity around what you are looking forward to in the conversation. Notice I didn't say what your agenda is. Eagerly anticipating what you are looking forward to correctly frames the conversation. This

Chapter 5: The Art of the Meeting

signals to your guest that you've done your homework and are ready.

If you've done your homework, a warm welcome is easy. It will typically complement your guest by acknowledging something unique to them. Here are a few "warm welcome" examples from meetings I've recently had:

- o *I noticed that you just opened a new location for your third studio. Congratulations!*

- o *I had not realized that you attended school in Italy. What an amazing experience that must have been!*

- o *Congratulations on the article in the Post. Your point on (x,y,z) was really well put ...*

As the conversation begins to warm up around a good welcome, that's when you provide clarity. Here are a few examples of how you might frame the conversation.

- o *Thanks again for meeting with me, Rob. You know, as I mentioned on our phone call, I'm really*

Find Your Six

> *eager to know more about ... (Advice/Particular Insight)*

o *Susan, as I was thinking about our conversation today, I must say that I was really looking forward to hearing about your company to understand (Particular Insight/How you may be able to help)*

You'll notice that your framing of the conversation in person can be, and is most often, a harkening back to the reasons to meet that you established in your call or email to set up the meeting. Once the conversation is kicked off in the right direction, your chances of fruitful connection are exponentially greater.

Listening for Clues

What you listen for as the conversation unfolds is as important as the questions you ask. Great questions unlock great conversation. It's here that the deeper themes emerge about how people think, how they attack problems, what drives them. These are the clues to finding influencers. It's also where the three influential characteristics we touched on in chapter three are put

Chapter 5: The Art of the Meeting

into action: longevity, fiduciary trust, and an ownership mindset.

It should be obvious by this point that I'm not a fan of teaching scripts. These deeply human conversations have to be entirely natural and therefore entirely yours. But that doesn't mean you should go into these conversations flying blind. I want to give you suggestions for the kinds of things you might say, but equally important guidance about what you should be asking yourself in the background—the reflective questions. As a great interviewer of talent, you'll need a strong degree of reflection to unlock the clues for which you are looking. Here are the influencer characteristics and clues in their answers that signify you are getting warmer finding your peak influencers:

Characteristic 1: Longevity

How do you determine whether someone has "longevity"? I've found it helpful to think of the concept of longevity as a combination of self-mastery and perseverance. It's the ability of professionals to stay the course year after year serving clients, constantly honing

Find Your Six

their craft, and increasing their overall influence. The self-mastery that this requires is considerable. Longevity understood this way can be observed in the little ways professionals approach their life.

Below are questions (Q) and the corresponding clues (C) you are looking for in your influencer candidate answers.

Q1. Are there any parts of your work you feel you've really mastered to achieve your success?

C1. Have they mastered a few things really well in order to have big results? <u>How</u> have they done this in their career?

Q2. Have you had any success in niche markets? (Suggest a few from your research)

C2. Are they strategic in their thinking? Do they approach business with a sporting, entrepreneurial spirit?

Q3. Do you have a specific morning routine that allows you to get so much done?

Chapter 5: The Art of the Meeting

C3. What and who do they prioritize above other things, and how do they achieve balance? What do they say no to habitually? How do they determine when to say yes? Do they routinely do what others see as difficult? Do they stretch themselves habitually?

Characteristic 2: Fiduciary Trust

The type of trust that influencers have is really a combination of their humility and the exceptional judgment they are able to offer their clients. Think about it: it's just not possible to put the needs of others ahead of yours without true humility and a track record of making wise decisions. To find this combination, here's what to look for in the dance of your conversation. As you read these, keep in mind that you are in the talent game, sifting out the "run it" types from the "own it" influencers:

Q1. Where do you see your business/yourself in three years?

Find Your Six

C1. Are they in the habit of constantly learning or have they "arrived" and know everything? Are they stagnant or growing?

Q2. Who are some of the people who have been most impactful on your career?

C2. Do they talk about themselves more than they express curiosity and admiration for others? Are they generous? Do they give of their time, talent, wealth?

Q3. Where (or to whom) have you gone for advice in growing your career/business?

C3. What serves as their internal moral compass that guides their decisions? Do they have mentors or respected advisors on whom they can rely for advice and accountability? What lessons have they picked up from their advisors? Do they make really wise decisions in all areas of life?

Chapter 5: The Art of the Meeting

Characteristic 3: Ownership Mindset

The ancient Greeks had a far more elegant word for an ownership mindset than we do today. It was *megalopsychia*—the habit of striving for great things. The modern English version is magnanimity. When people own their role with this magnanimous spirit, we appreciate it immediately. As we've seen, those with an ownership mindset fundamentally approach life and business from an angle that makes them magnanimous. Here's what you are looking for:

Q1. What personal goals do you have for your (career/work/company)?

C1. Are they abundant thinkers or scarce thinkers? Do they have a necessarily optimistic vision for themselves and do they doggedly pursue it?

Q2. How do you find the right people to bring into your (team/board/company)? Do you have a methodology for making sure you have a great match?

Find Your Six

C2. Do they see great potential in others, or does it seem as if they depend entirely on their personal talents? Are they interested in forming those around them?

Q3. What has been the biggest failure you've encountered in the business?

C3. Do they make excuses for their failures or the missteps of their organization or does the buck stop with them?

If finding individuals with these qualities seems like a tall order, you are absolutely correct. Those who are profoundly trusted, blame no one except themselves for their failures, and stay the course when others throw in the towel are actually quite unique. To be sure, no one is perfect, but perfection is not what you are looking for. Nonetheless, influence depends on what I characterize as heroic human qualities, and when you know what to look for, you'll turn influence up in places you never would have anticipated.

Chapter 5: The Art of the Meeting

The Law of Reciprocity

It's important to note that great conversations and relationships are reciprocal. If it's all about you, even if your product or service or presentation is top-shelf, you won't win over the influencer candidates. When you are interested in their business—how you can help them, how they have found success, what they are struggling with, how they find clients, and the like—you will have a much more authentic, interesting and fruitful relationship. When influencers understand how you conduct yourself professionally, you occupy a place in their mind as someone they can endorse because of how you are impacting their business.

One of my mentors once told me that the questions you ask are the questions that you will receive. Applied to your conversations with influencer candidates, the lesson is that the better your questions are, the better the questions you will receive in return. Great questions cause deep and creative thought. People who have a high degree of emotional intelligence (which is most certainly an attribute of influencers and leaders) reciprocate

Find Your Six

questions. Since it's not about them, influencers will have developed a keen sense of curiosity for those around them, and they will ask you questions in return. The better your questions to an influencer, the more inspired the influencer will be to ask you insightful, authentically curious questions in return. (It wouldn't hurt to have answers to the questions you are asking them at the ready.)

When you ask the right questions and you have the right talent in front of you, influencer candidates almost always see you as someone they could put their name to—someone with whom they would be proud to be associated. When this happens, their world of relationships begins to open to you. We don't open our relationships to just anyone. I don't get to hang out with your kids or friends and family or your business associates or clients without first winning your trust. And you won't know if you can trust me until you understand how I think. There are few better ways to show someone how you think than the questions you ask. The dance begins on the right foot with the right questions, but it gets really interesting when reciprocity

Chapter 5: The Art of the Meeting

happens. The questions you answer when influencers reciprocate with their own questions will solidify what they suspected—you really are cut from a different cloth. That's how the dance works.

When reciprocity happens, it allows for true dialogue. Dialogue only happens when there is a trusting give and take from both sides. The back and forth of dialogue is present between mentee and mentor. It needs to be in play if you ever hope to create the influencer relationships that happen as a result of your meetings and well-crafted questions. Dialogue, both conversationally and figuratively, is the goal.

Simply put, in addition to identifying influencers, a primary goal of your meeting is to produce more meetings. More meetings happen because you ask the right questions to the right people. Those right people reciprocate, and real conversational dialogue builds the trust necessary for them to put you in front of their influencers. This is what Gerry did for me in that first meeting. He connected me.

Find Your Six

Wrapping Up the Meeting

Just as you began the meeting with the gift of good questions, you need to end the meeting with a good question. At the end of a good meeting, I would say something along these lines:

o *Knowing what you know about me and my business at this point, if you were me, who else would you sit down with?*

Or

o *Based on what you know about my business, is there anyone else you think I should speak to who could give me advice?*

Now it's not uncommon that before the end of the meeting influencers who are really dynamic connectors will already have mentioned some names of people with whom they think you'd be interested in connecting. Naturally, you wouldn't ask this question if this was the case. Instead, you would say something like:

Chapter 5: The Art of the Meeting

o   *I really appreciate you thinking to connect me with Phil. What do you think is the best way for me to get in touch with him?*

What you are looking for in each of these questions is an action item. You are looking for someone to take action and connect you.

There is no better way to get connected to an influencer's table than to connect the influencer to yours. When this system becomes your business development arm, you will have an ever-growing mental database of people who are influencers (or candidates) at the ready in the back of your mind. As a conversation unfolds and you see that someone from your contacts will be of value to the person in front of you, you might say something like:

o   *Do you happen to know Anna Greenwald at BlueSpark? She's one of the best CPAs I've ever dealt with. If you'd like, I'd be thrilled to make a connection for you.*

145

Find Your Six

Then at the end of the meeting you'll say:

o *When I get back to my desk, I'll send an email introducing you to Anna. I think you'll really enjoy meeting her.*

At this point, it's not uncommon for good influencer candidates to immediately mention someone they want to connect you to. It's even more common that, when they get back to the office and have thought about your conversation, they will fire off an email either to ask you if a certain person would be a good introduction for you or simply to connect you directly to them.

Some meetings that you have will yield two or three other meetings. But let's get conservative on the numbers. What if, on average, you connect each person you meet with to one other strong contact, and each person you meet with connects you to just one other person you can meet with? You would never run out of people to meet with. And because over time you will only hone the art of your meetings—asking great questions, causing reciprocity and dialogue, and connecting great people—

Chapter 5: The Art of the Meeting

you will build a network of fantastic professionals as you find your peak influencers.

You can't get any of this if you are in the business of finding how you can get people to give you things. This is not a scripted sale; instead, it's a human investment. Human beings are incredibly adept at knowing when they're being sold to and when they are being given a gift. For influencers and people who aspire to be influencers, the greatest gift they can receive is wisdom. The greatest vehicle for wisdom that I have found in business are wise people. That's why it's completely accurate to say that you're in the talent business—because wisdom resides in high-level talent. In the game of influence, if you can be a wisdom distributor, you win.

While the best vehicle for distributing wisdom is talented people, they are not the only vehicle. As a rule, even when I'm speaking with someone I determine is not an influencer candidate, I still want to give that person the gift of wisdom. Personally, I like sending people books or even a TED Talk or an article that applies to their specific needs. The point is this: if somebody dignifies you by accepting your invitation and spending

Find Your Six

time with you, you owe them. Sure, you could give a Starbucks gift card or some chocolate, but you're not in the chocolate or coffee business. If you want to be associated with high-level client care, don't give what anyone else can give: commodities. Instead, give the only thing that can't be commoditized: wisdom.

If you don't have someone in mind you can connect the person to, at the end of a meeting you should make a note of a book that you think might be good for that person or look up a pertinent article. This requires that you become an expert in the fields that you are speaking about. If you're asking business questions you need to become a business expert. You have to be immersed in the resources that will be effective for business owners of all shapes and sizes. The greater the influence you want to surround yourself with, the greater your own store of wisdom needs to become. In order to do this, I almost always ask successful people what books they recommend. You can build a pretty amazing library just by asking for book recommendations.

Chapter 5: The Art of the Meeting

Influencer Profile:
Dr. Siri Terjesen

Being a wisdom distributor is a direct result of the network of exceptional professionals with which you align yourself. Professionals who focus on wisdom distribution to their network are simultaneously a sparkplug for growth for the people they connect as well as a magnet for influencers through whom they can grow their professional career. Over time the radical impact on a career can be nothing short of massive. Wisdom distribution works like compounding interest, quickly increasing your ability to write your own ticket to success. In every profession I've ever observed, wisdom distributors far outpace their competition's professsional growth because they have an undeniable asset that the rest of the market would love to have, even if they can't put their finger on it.

I met Dr. Siri Terjesen while she was the director of American University's Center for Innovation and benefited almost immediately from her personal influence as well as her network of influencers. It seemed no sooner had she realized how she could

Find Your Six

help me and how I might help her network that connections were made. Siri is one of the most natural wisdom distributors I've ever encountered.

As it turns out, early in her career as a graduate student, Siri consciously began finding the best mentors she could. But she didn't stop there. She found a way to collaborate with these mentors to help their careers grow as well. She's written books with some and helped others find new positions, teaching assistants, or academic collaborators as a result of her ever-growing network. Because of her constant and habitual investment into her network, Siri not only enjoys an amazing professional reputation as a professor who is a wisdom distributor for her students, but she's also known for her ability to introduce vision-aligned donors to the institutions where she teaches. This combination of business developer and well-regarded academic has allowed Siri to have her choice of career path. When it came time to make a move so she had more time to golf with her kids, she had her pick of positions and chose to move to Florida Atlantic University and become their Associate Dean in the School of Business.

Chapter 5: The Art of the Meeting

In a higher education marketplace where enrollment at universities is declining and tenure no longer ensures job stability, the ability to write your own ticket is increasingly valuable to say the least.

Conclusion

The goal for me as a real estate agent was always to have the person across the table from me think (and sometimes even vocalize) something like this: "Wow—I thought you were just a real estate agent!" When you can cause this reaction, you are winning over advocates for your business. The only question left once you have advocates is how influential they are.

What would your business look like if you were a connector and advisor for businesses? Someone on whom others called for advice because of your track record of finding solutions? An implicitly trusted board advisor? We all know people like this. They are the individuals who are constantly sought after for their advice—the influencers who spend most of their day, well, influencing.

Find Your Six

Being humble and insightful enough to make the ask, diligent enough to do the research, curious enough to have great meetings, and invested enough to be a wisdom distributor is the art that Siri, Ben and so many others who take control of their professional destiny have mastered. In so doing, they have become influencers in an ever-expanding curated network of talent. The final element that they have mastered in this influencer art is *keeping* their most valuable influencer relationships ever-expanding and thus ever more influential.

Chapter 6
A TABLE FOR SIX

"Trust no one unless you have eaten much salt with him."

MARCUS TULLIUS CICERO

I want to make an outlandish but not unanticipated claim at the outset of this final chapter: that in order to radically alter the course of your business (and perhaps your life) all you need is to find six influencers.

That's it: just six.

Find Your Six

Six influencers and you have a foundation upon which you can build wealth, enormous success, and even a business that you can pass on once you are ready to teach others your craft.

You have probably heard the following quote (most often attributed to the life coach Jim Rohn): "You are the average of the five people you spend the most time with." Maybe you've also heard the adage "show me your friends and I'll show you your future." Whether the number is 5 or 7 and whether it's friends or business influencers, the fact is when you apply this perennial knowledge to your business, you begin to control the future of your business in amazing ways. In short, if you can find your 6, you'll soon discover (as I explain below) that six is just a starting point.

Any time I make this claim there is some degree of disbelief. It would seem that with all of the work you've put in and all of the people you know that you would have *already* found your six. The fact is, most of us have been at the right party working diligently to connect, endear ourselves, win friends and influence people...

Chapter 6: A Table for Six

but we've just been at the wrong table. The right table makes all the difference.

Seating Arrangements

Say you are invited to a fancy fundraiser at which you are served dinner. You might think to yourself that this is going to be a great chance to grow your professional database. You find your table which the host committee has determined for you in advance. It's a round-top seating eight guests. As you pick your seat, you see that you don't know a soul at the table. *No problem* you think to yourself—*I make friends easily!* As you introduce yourself to the other guests, the DJ cranks up the music, making it hard to even hear the names of your would-be friends. The noise is accompanied by busy waiters who come to take your orders: "Would you like the beef, chicken or the veggie option?" You graciously thank the waiter—beef it is. And what the heck—you grab a dinner roll too.

As you pass the rolls, you notice that the guest to your left has run off to the table next door to commiserate with

Find Your Six

an old friend from her college days. The person to your right is immersed in the glow of his phone, checking social media, dead to the world around him. Then there's the person on the opposite side of the table sitting by herself, taking it all in. You make eye contact and smile around the centerpiece and mouth "nice to meet you" but you both realize that trying to have a real conversation is unrealistic. She stretches to hand you a business card. At best you have some polite exchanges with the guests once dinner starts. You play the name game with someone who lives in a small town your best friend is from. You compliment the suit of another who goes into a five-minute monologue about how he never wears suits anymore.

At least the food was good.

The next day your mom calls to check-in. She asks who you sat with ... and you draw a total blank: "Thanks for asking, Mom ... but I couldn't tell you."

Too many people are trying to make connections at tables like the one I've described. Everyone at the table is a perfectly nice person, but the likelihood of any of them

Chapter 6: A Table for Six

becoming a peak influencer for you is about the same as finding the proverbial needle in a haystack.

Now imagine another table. You are in a private room at the back of a restaurant that you booked. You have personally invited the people around the table, carefully selecting them. Each of them is someone you know well on a business level and some of them you know quite well on a personal level. The barely noticeable music is just high enough to ensure the privacy of your group's conversation. The waiter doesn't rush or interrupt you or the others in the room. The guests' attention is undivided and they are excited to be there because of who you are or who you could be to them and their businesses.

Over the course of your meal, you foster conversations between people at the table, pointing out opportunities for them to work together, benefit one another and trade ideas about business. Most of these business owners did not know the others at the table before this meal. By the end of your time together each of them knows who they are sitting with and are grateful that you offered them the opportunity to meet. Many of them have already decided

Find Your Six

to meet up again, make introductions for each other or even do business together. You've instigated thousands of dollars of potential value for every person at the table—and they in turn can't wait to return the favor.

The interplay of influencers at the top of the pyramid is like this second table. When you find the right peak influencers, it's not enough to simply keep in touch. Instead, if you want this dance to continue, you will need to help them continue to grow their influence.

Whether you are building a tech startup, recruiting for the New York Yankees or having friends over for dinner, who you invite to join you as you play the game of business and life makes all the difference.

Just like creating your first list and having the right meetings, setting your table for this type of success does not happen accidentally. It's strategic and completely on purpose.

Chapter 6: A Table for Six

THE SECOND TABLE

Pounds or Rubles?

I've used the three-level pyramid image to illustrate who true influencers are and the power of having true influence for your business. Let's go back to the influencer pyramid one last time to add a finishing touch. I've found it is also very useful in seeing how to invest in influencers—and conversely what falls short. It turns out that influencers require an altogether distinct

Find Your Six

type of investment. Wisdom distributors like Ben and Siri are masters of making the strategic investment deposits into the right people, yielding them and their fellow influencers massive returns on their investment.

The measure of an investment is what you are able to receive as a result of the investment. When thinking about human investments and the impact on your business, the return on investment is determined by the positive result we desire: an order, a referral, a signed client, a new and valuable connection. We make deposits in people with the hope that we can build trust with each of them so that they do business with us.

As seen earlier, we often fall into the trap of looking for the same result from every portion of our pyramid. What's the evidence for this? We make deposits into everyone in the pyramid in the same way. That's what lead generation does: it defaults to treating everyone we know or could know as having the same potential for our business—and it therefore uses the same general tactics across all of them. But what should be clear by now is that what you need to deposit when dealing with influencers is unique at the top of the pyramid, because

Chapter 6: A Table for Six

influencers are a different breed entirely. Trying to make business happen at the top with the same tactics you use for folks at the bottom or middle of the pyramid is like trying to buy lunch in London with rubles from Russia when what you really need (and the only money the restaurant will take) are pounds sterling.

Are you in the business of making deposits that return at a positive response rate of fifty-to-one (think rubles), or are you in a 2-to-1 or better business (pounds sterling)? Put another way: is it one deposit for every one positive response (order, referral, signed client) or is it 50-to-1 (or worse)[1]?

Traditional marketing campaigns are *lucky* to yield a 50-to-1 return. You can look at them in two different ways to come to the same realization:

o You eed to touch at least 50 people to sell one product or deal.

o You need to touch the same person 50 times to get them to do business with you.

---

[1] As of this writing, one Pound Sterling equals 104.61 Russian Rubles.

Find Your Six

Cold calling, online lead campaigns, door knocking, and canned mailings to past clients all have at best a 50-to-1 return, but usually much worse. At the bottom of the pyramid, you are trying to generate business with rubles. You are at the wrong table. You want to be at the table that's dealing in sterling.

In the middle of the pyramid, the method of investment is still distinct from the top of the pyramid. While you may market to these folks, you are also able to send them frequent business. The value of a closed deal for someone you refer can be very significant, clearly worth more to them than a cold call or your slick marketing piece. And just to reiterate a concept from earlier in the book: because of the relative value that we assign to these referrals, we assume that when such a big deposit is made, it will yield a much higher return than what we actually receive when dealing with the middle of the pyramid. In other words, because we are dealing in referrals, it feels as though we went from having rubles to pounds, only to realize that we're only working with Canadian dollars—perfectly fine for most people, but still not pounds sterling (let's not forget that Canadians

Chapter 6: A Table for Six

fondly refer to their dollar coins as "loonies"). You are again trading in the wrong marketplace.

In the middle of the pyramid the investment to return ratio is about a 25-to-1 ratio. That's 25 referrals of business to one closed deal for you. It's here where a lot of frustration can boil up if you don't recognize that you are doing business in the middle. You can really enjoy working with these people and they are probably excellent at their jobs, but in spite of how you feel about them, they simply are not able to directly generate massive growth for your business. You are still at the wrong table, though oftentimes you fail to recognize that that's the case.

Which brings us back to the top of the pyramid: it's here where you finally find pounds sterling in play. It's here where what you bring is not only valued, but that value is responded to with the best returns you can get.

Here's something else about this table: you can't show up to it with marketing. It would fall flat. "What are you doing with those rubles at this table?" the people would say. Nor can you show up with an elevator pitch. Influencers will just tune you out and check their phones.

Find Your Six

You can only show up to this carefully curated table with pounds sterling. When you trade as a wisdom distributor for influencers and do it well, your investment yields a two-to-one return or better. That's as good as it gets in any business. When this is your table, every other form of business development—especially lead gen—feels like a distraction at best.

And you only get this table by setting it yourself.

RELATIONAL INVESTMENT RATIOS

Chapter 6: A Table for Six

The Hockey Stick

What's interesting about being at the right table is that the right relationships have a way of becoming not just helpful with referrals in the short term, but they also act like a good mutual fund—compounding the interest of your investment over time. What do you suppose is the most natural result of inviting guests to your table, serving them the best connections, business insights, and authentic interest in their business?

They invite you to their table.

That's right—you're not the only influencer with a table of your own. And this is where your search for the right six relationships expands to turn into 12, 18, 24 . . .

Your focus on the top of the pyramid is not just trading pounds sterling in London for a sandwich. It's trading in pounds sterling on the London Stock Exchange. It's a true investment.

Find Your Six

THE IMPACT OF INVITATIONS
TO YOUR INFLUENCERS' TABLES

In their book *The One Thing,* Garry Keller and Jay Papasan pose a simple yet powerful focusing question based on the great economist Vilfredo Pareto's 80/20 principle: *What is the one thing I can do such that everything else becomes easier or not necessary?* The answer when it comes to the lessons of business development I've proposed in this book should be incredibly clear:

Find your six.

Chapter 6: A Table for Six

When you find your six, everything else becomes easier. Instead of lead generation, throwing rubles around, and playing a pure numbers game, your focus in setting the table for influence creates efficiencies that grow your business, grow your professional advisors— and perhaps most importantly—deeply impact who you become over time: an influencer yourself.

This focus on a few key players works in the same way that compounding interest works. As you invest, you see modest returns at first, but the discipline of making investments regularly over time goes from modest to massive returns very suddenly. If you've ever seen a chart of how interest compounds, it looks almost unbelievable—truly magical. It's said that even Albert Einstein marveled at the miracle of compounding interest: "Compound interest is the eighth wonder of the world. He who understands it, earns it. He who doesn't, pays it." Fortunately, it doesn't take Einstein's mind to understand that there is nothing miraculous here. Rather, all you need to realize is that compounding interest is mathematically inevitable—and that the miracle can happen when you find your six.

Find Your Six

As you make these far-sighted relationship investments in search of your six, a ripple effect will occur. In the short-term, business will happen. By virtue of connecting with great people and the way in which you connect to them, many will see you as a resource. You will be top of mind, and top of mind resources get business. You might think of this as the network effect. The resulting network (which tellingly is not the goal but just the result) will spin off business. Perhaps unsurprisingly, this network will be far more effective than any networking group you could have joined, because it's one thing to join networks but quite another to entirely build your own. Your connections will be automatically deeper and the way in which you are perceived will be categorically different than if you just show up to a table at a networking event. At your table, you are the host, controlling many more variables and adding exponentially more value to the conversation than when you are a guest.

In the middle term, you will find that it's never been easier to find potential candidates with whom to meet. Candidates you invest in will connect you to their tables

Chapter 6: A Table for Six

of influence, putting their good names to yours and insisting that you break bread with their influencers as well.

And finally, in the longer term, one by one, your peak influencers will begin to make a more significant impact, as their influencers connect you to their influencers, and so on. This is where your business will move from growing steadily to growing exponentially. It's the hockey stick effect. One table leads to another then another, creating first a three-legged stool, then a strong chair, then a scaffolding, and then a house built on a solid foundation.

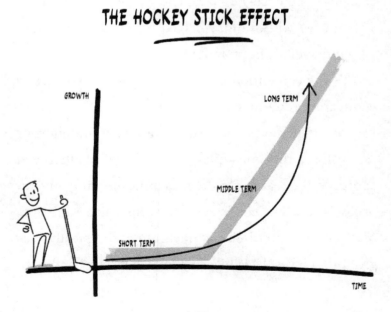

Find Your Six

This is how a practice turns into an asset—a true business. It's a business that is so solid that it can be sold or given to your kids to run—either way leaving a legacy for generations if you choose.

What is the lifetime career cost of not finding your six influencers for your table? And what's the generational impact of not finding your six?

The Six Month FY6 Challenge

I want to issue a challenge to you. Like any worthy challenge, there will be a clear end goal with a time limit. That way we will know if you have won or lost. Here it is:

Find your six in six months.

It's my contention that no matter where you are in your career you can do this.

Now that you know what the results of finding your six will be, the only question really is whether you approach the search for them as a meandering journey or a mission. The challenge is treating it like a mission. Meanderers won't build momentum and typically they give up as a result. While they may get lucky and even

Chapter 6: A Table for Six

have some above-average results on occasion, they will miss the opportunity for more aggressive returns.

Instead, I want you to deposit a big lump sum into your business quickly—in six months—so you can grow it aggressively.

And I'm not just going to challenge you to a big life-changing goal—I'm giving you the life-changing roadmap. Here it is:

Step 1: Block out three hours of time and make your list (see chapter 4's *Eating your Ego* and *Where to Start: Friends and Neighbors*).

Step 2: Begin setting up meetings and have at least one daily for five days every week. This comes out to about 20 meetings per month (see chapter 4's *The Three Categories of Acceptable Asks*).

Step 3: About twenty-five percent of these meetings will produce influencer candidate "matches." That means that on a per month basis, you will find five peak influencer "finalists." In six months, you will have found

171

Find Your Six

30 finalists (see chapter 5's *Doing Your Homework* and *The Reason You're Here*).

Step 4: Of these finalists, 20% will be true influencers for your business. Twenty percent of 30 candidates is *six* influencers (see chapter 5's *Listening for Clues* and *The Law of Reciprocity*).

This may sound like just a numbers game, but if you see this system as success by the numbers alone you haven't been reading closely enough. Everything I've said up to this point is about the *quality* of your interactions and not the quantity (after all, I'm talking about one meeting a day, not three). Taking a quantitative approach will mean you have a lot of meetings and *still* fail. You'll be a commodity and you won't develop the art of conversation. Your table will be set, but no one will be sitting down.

Art depends on the constant growth in a craft. This isn't paint by numbers. This is honing a skillset. The goal is not to "fake it" and make something that just imitates great art. Artistic imitation is a total commodity. This is

Chapter 6: A Table for Six

why you can purchase a print of Vincent van Gogh's work for a few dollars online.

Through the lessons of these chapters, I am proposing something else: I want you to achieve mastery. The mastery of the angler on the shores of an abundant river systematically focused on finding the right catch is far from any feeling that you need to lead generate to reach your goals. You already have the raw material to begin with because you can communicate. I don't care if you are charismatic or shy, what your sign is or what Myers-Briggs says about you. There are no other great gifts needed to become masterful at finding your six: just the belief that the journey is worth embarking upon and the anticipation of sitting at the top surrounded by great influencers.

Go find your six!

Find Your Six

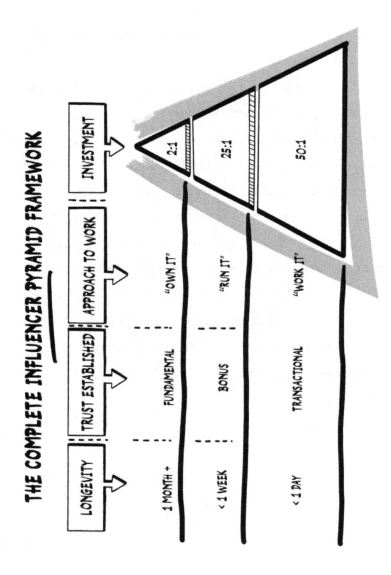

EPILOGUE

The first year is always the hardest. The year that John came into my business was no exception. When the stakes are high, it follows that stress also spikes. It's what you do with that stress that determines your outcomes in business and in life more generally.

That first year, driven by the high stakes, John and I worked at a breakneck pace. We met with every potential candidate we could think of, invested into them with wisdom—books, contacts, analysis that we crafted for their specific circumstances—and did everything we could legally think of to help their businesses grow. I'd like to say it was easy once we put in the time, but it wasn't: it was a messy process. But I suppose nothing is perfect, especially when you are trying to teach it for the first time. We made deposits into people who wasted our time, confused folks with a "work it" mindset for those with an "own it" mindset, and forgot to follow up with great candidates. We failed at our process as much as we

Find Your Six

succeeded. Luckily, we saw the mess for what it was and we created a way to turn our failures into a better and better process.

Every week, we had a meeting to wade through the mess. We would ask two simple questions: What's working? And what's not? We would look at every meeting we had and figure out how to refine our questions, how to find better candidates and, most importantly, who was likely to rise to the top of our pyramid. This weekly meeting kept us moving forward through the mess we were making.

By the end of the year, we could see the beginning of the hockey stick effect. Our investments into influencers were beginning to pay off and, in the meantime, just enough revenue was coming in to keep food on our tables and to keep from taking on more debt.

At the end of his third full year in the business, John had sold more homes in the previous 12 months than any other agent in Montgomery County, Maryland (a large suburb of Washington, DC and one of the most competitive markets in the US). Total revenue for my business had more than doubled.

Epilogue

Eight years later and many more relationships forged, John is now my business partner. Our team does over $80 million dollars in annual volume and growing even as our competition gets squeezed out of the business in the disruption that is changing the residential real estate marketplace daily.

What's more gratifying still is how our business has grown as a result of finding and investing into the right six year after year. There's a profound joy that has come as a result of the many long-term influencers who continue to see us as a resource to them, their clients, friends and family. We wouldn't have it any other way.

You only get to run the race once. Who you run with makes all the difference.

ABOUT THE AUTHOR

Patrick Kilner is a husband and a father first and a business owner second. As such he has obsessively and systematically designed his businesses to be entirely at the service of his family. This includes the system that you will find in this book.

When not writing, Pat spends his time leading companies (mostly in real estate), training driven people (mostly in service industries), and volunteering on nonprofit boards (mostly in education).

Pat and his wife, Elena have eight children. Pat wrote this book over the course of a year between the hours of 4 and 6 AM.

To take the *Find Your Six* challenge,
access free resources,
and join the FY6 movement,
visit FindYourSix.com.